ENDORSEMENTS

"Maxine Marsolini has written a raw and powerful story of an abusive mother and a son who yearns to overcome the wounds inflicted upon him as a child. It's a sometimes ugly, but always realistic, portrayal of an abused child and how those wounds affect his life even as an adult. Written sometimes in the second person but also in the words of the abused, Marsolini incorporates excellent strategies at the end of each chapter for both abusers and the abused. This unique book is destined to help many of the most hurting in our culture."

— **Rick Johnson, bestselling author of *Becoming Your Spouse's Better Half* and *The Power of a Man***

"Maxine Marsolini has introduced us to an almost unimaginable world of horror in her book: *A Mother's Fury*. Sadly, the story of Charles Rice, which is told in the book, is not fiction, and it is not as rare as we might hope. Child abuse and neglect is a cancerous reality in our neighborhoods, and is carried forward generation after generation by those who were themselves first innocent victims. The abuse and neglect they suffered was the template given to them of how parents are expected to interact with their own children.

However awful the realities of child abuse are, there still remains hope for the victims, both young and old, and this is the powerful message Ms. Marsolini bring to us in her book.

At the close of each chapter, are exercises designed to open the doors to healing and freedom from the pain of childhood abuse. Solidly anchored in the truth of Scripture, and in good therapeutic activities, the opportunity is presented for the reader to begin the journey to wholeness.

This book can serve well as a starting point for discussions and interventions to enable and empower the victims to step forward onto a path of forgiveness and healing in a nurturing relationship with God.

While many victims of childhood abuse will need professional help beyond the scope of this book, I strongly believe that *A Mother's Fury* is a valuable and important statement that hope and healing can be found for the victims still suffering from the wounds of their childhoods."

— James R. Baker, M.A., CADC-1

"My first book, *Out of Control*, told how God delivered me from being a child abuser. Maxine Marsolini's book looks at the problem of child abuse from the child's viewpoint and it is a powerful, compelling, and yes, painful book, but oh, so very, very needed. I wish it had been available when I was struggling with abusive anger. I believe it would have helped me. I feared I was ruining my child's life but I also believed God no longer loved me. Marsolini includes help for both the abused child and the abuser. I trust it will help others know there is healing for that child and there is God's faithful love and power for that abuser. There was for me and my child. Today, we share a fabulous relationship!

— **Kathy Collard Miller, speaker and author of** *Never, Never, Never Be The Same*
Congratulations!
Kathy
www.KathyCollardMiller.blogspot.com

MOTHER'S FURY

RELEASING THE TRAUMA
OF CHILDHOOD ABUSE

MAXINE MARSOLINI

Copyright ©2015-2016 by Maxine Marsolini

2015-2016 Ellechor Publishing House Edition
Mother's Fury: Releasing the Trauma of Childhood Abuse / Maxine Marsolini

Paperback ISBN13: 978-1-937844-20-2

No portion of this book may be reproduced, scanned, or distributed in any form without the written permission of the Publisher. Please purchase only authorized editions. For more information, address:

Ellechor Media, LLC
2373 NW 185th Ave, #510
Hillsboro, OR 97124
info@ellechormedia.com

If you purchased this book without a cover, you should be aware that this book is stolen property. It was reported as "unsold" or "destroyed" to the publisher, and neither the author nor the publisher has received any payment for this "stripped book."

Unless otherwise noted, all Scripture is from THE HOLY BIBLE, NEW INTERNATIONAL VERSION®, NIV® Copyright © 1973, 1978, 1984, 2011 by Biblica, Inc.® Used by permission. All rights reserved worldwide.

Scripture quotations marked NLT are taken from the Holy Bible, New Living Translation, copyright © 1996, 2004, 2007 by Tyndale House Foundation. Used by permission of Tyndale House Publishers, Inc., Carol Stream, Illinois 60188. All rights reserved.

Scripture quotations marked NKJV are taken from the New King James Version®. Copyright © 1982 by Thomas Nelson, Inc. Used by permission. All rights reserved.

Scripture quotations marked MSG are taken from The Message. Copyright © 1993, 1994, 1995, 1996, 2000, 2001, 2002. Used by permission of NavPress Publishing Group.

Cover & Interior Design by D.E. West, Ellechor Publishing House / ZAQ Designs

Printed in the United States of America

www.ellechorpublishinghouse.com

This book sets out to tackle the difficult subject of mother abuse in a constructive way. While the story is true, the help given is not intended to replace or prevent the reader from seeking other forms of professional counsel or treatment. The author assumes no liability for how this material is put into practice.

DEDICATION

Thank you, Charles Rice, for sharing your story. You know firsthand what it means to live with a volatile mother. I am aware that those memories ushered in tears and triggered flashbacks. They testified to wounds that ran deep and cried out to be released. No child should ever experience such grievous wrongs and bear such devastating pain.

Unfortunately, we live in a world where sin exists and bad things do happen to children. The choice to move beyond a mother's fury took courage. However, in that momentous act of courage to move forward—to that place of letting go, you found the fresh air of freedom's balm to soothe your dreadful past. Your voice will help other victims of childhood abuse release their own trauma.

It is my prayer that those raised under the heavy hand of an abusive mother will move beyond their sufferings to discover how very real God's love is. Beloved child, you are the apple of His eye. The God, who gave you life, loves you with an everlasting, never-ending, immeasurable love.

> *"Can a mother forget the baby at her breast and*
> *have no compassion the child she has bone?*
> *Though she may forget, I will not forget you!"*
> Isaiah 49:15 NIV

> *Sometimes life is so atrocious that surviving is its*
> *own great achievement and a strange proof*
> *of sorts that God must exist.*[1]
> — Beth Moore

CONTENTS

Dedication ix
Foreword xiii
Introduction xv

ONE: I'll Never Forget! 3
TWO: "Mommy, Where's Daddy?" 19
THREE: All Hell Exploded Around Me 37
FOUR: The Last Two Years of High School 55
FIVE: Invited to Church 75
SIX: Finding My Father 85
SEVEN: Mother's New Hobby 97
EIGHT: "I'm Outta Here!" 115
NINE: Dealt Another Dirty Card 129
TEN: Surprised! 147
ELEVEN: Truth and Generosity 165
TWELVE: Shattered Dreams 181
THIRTEEN: Letting Go 207

ONE MORE THING 217
THE GOAL: God's Design for a Woman 221
ENDNOTES 227
NATIONAL STATISTICS ON CHILD ABUSE ... 229
ADDENDUM: Resources 233
RECOMMENDED READING 235
ACKNOWLEDGEMENTS 239
ABOUT THE AUTHOR 241

FOREWORD

It's difficult for many of us to realize that mothers can be so damaged themselves that they inflict immeasurable pain on their children. This is the story of Charles, an emotionally and physically abused son, who constantly tries to appease an unappeasable mother. Marsolini provides frequent pauses for self-reflection for the abused, the abuser, and for anyone who seeks a greater measure of hope and joy in life.

— Cecil Murphey is the author or co-author of 137 books such as *90 Minutes in Heaven* and *Gifted Hands: the Ben Carson Story*. Two of his books deal with the sexual abuse and pain of boys: *When a Man You Love Was Abused* and *Not Quite Healed*. He also writes a confidential blog, *www.menshatteringthesilence.blogspot.com*

INTRODUCTION

*Even as a small child of five or six, I began
to dread and even hate the weekends. I knew that
was when I was in the most danger of being beaten, kicked,
deprived of food, locked in my room, and anything else my
mother's depraved mind could conceive.*
— Charles Rice

This might read like a horror story, but it's true. There's a real person in serious peril with a desperate need to escape from insurmountable odds. How does a powerless child survive emotional and physical pain day after day, year after year? The Charles Rice story is used as the backdrop to expose what happens to a child when Mommy, the primary caregiver, is furious and unsafe. Home for these children is a dark and frightening world. How do they break free? How do they feel good about who they are—or know they have value? And how does growing up with abuse impact the quality of future relationships? Could they, too, become abusers?

This book speaks to the physical, emotional, verbal, and neglect maltreatment of children. It does not address sexual abuse. Pages tell of horrific parenting and vulgar profanity acted out upon a child who would never know what it was like to feel safe in the presence of his own mother.

Charles's story begins with the vivid memory of the day his parents' divorce became final. Daddy was moving out and never coming home. Not wanting this to happen, he burst into a torrent of unstoppable tears. He ran after the car, screaming, "Daddy don't go! Come back!" His father never came back—not even for a visit. What happened next would explode emotions in a thousand different directions.

It's reported that 40.5% of all child abuse is committed by biological mothers. Despite their ability to function well on the job, or in the presence of other adults, the majority of abusers are mothers who, behind closed doors, rage at their own children.

According to the statistics included at the end of this book under the heading "National Statistics on Child Abuse," approximately 681,000 children were victims of maltreatment in 2011 alone. Nearly five children die every day in America from abuse and neglect. In 2011, an estimated 1,570 children died from abuse and neglect. In the same year, Children's Advocacy Centers around the country served more than 279,000 child victims of abuse, providing victim advocacy and support to these children and their families. In 2012, this number was nearly 287,000. Clearly, the problem is a significant one. Read the entire report on page 229.

It's inconceivable for most of us to imagine a mother as a source of dread or the villain in a nightmare. Mothers are typically associated with feelings of love and trust—nurturers, not monsters. But cruelty knows no gender, and some parents do harm their defenseless children.

Where is God? He's crying, too. God's nature is love and He loves you so very much. However, the potential to do evil exists in all of us. It's part of our sinful nature. Just as there are wonderful dads and abusive dads, there are also extraordinary moms and those who bully and batter their children. Raging parents can be nice and sweet one minute and explosive the next. Their unpredictability is what's most unsettling and dangerous. While Charles's mother caused his tears and inflicted undeserved pain, some hot-tempered moms wipe away tears and even kiss skinned knees.

To their credit, a large number of abusers do hate how they treat their children but don't know how to disclose such an awful secret or seek help to step out from behind the shame. As a result, they stay trapped in a never-ending cycle of abuse and all too often raise children who also become abusers. Childhood abuse victims are 1,000 times more likely to also abuse. Does this fit you or someone you know?

The pages of this book aim to set the wounded free and to break through the repetitive nature of child abuse while giving the rest of us a growing awareness and empathy for a hurting group of people. Abuse against children is wrong. Collectively, we can help end the cruelty and save lives.

Victims of child abuse are the main focus, but abusers are people, too. Both need help to recognize and stop the maltreatment from continuing. The author is a life coach, not a licensed therapist. Her intent is to generate courage within the reader; courage to take the lid off shame-filled secrets while leaving the assurance of being fully loved behind. Where God's grace is plentiful, it's not unusual for once-difficult relationships to find ample room to chart a new course.

As portions of individual stories emerge, past hurts no longer dictate who people are or who they will become. This is a story that rises from the scars to deliver a path forward.

Now, more than four decades after making his bold, covert escape from the home he tagged the Hornet's Nest, Charles Rice has set free the man who, as a small boy, dared not express his feelings. For too many years, he had cowered in fear, silenced his thoughts, and focused on simply surviving one moment to the next. But the day came when he knew it was important to face what happened to him and move toward emotional healing. His story will stir others to take that same giant step. Victims will discover there is a way to let go, forgive, and grab hold of fresh joy. Life can be happy . . . and safe . . . and fulfilling in spite of what has been endured.

Chapters are followed by optional growth sections. *Reach for Fresh Joy* strives to help the abused mend. *Reach for Fresh Hope* will prompt the abuser to deal with abusive behaviors and assimilate appropriate parenting skills. Some readers may use both sections.

You may wish the expression of anger in your family had been different. It wasn't then. It may not be now. You cannot change your past experiences by pretending they didn't happen . . . But you can change their effect and continued expression in your own life. It's your choice.[2]

— Gary Jackson Oliver and H. Norman Wright

ONE

I'LL NEVER FORGET!

I first met Charles Rice while filming a parenting series for a TV station. He was one of the cameramen that day. My family talks had hit a raw nerve in Charles's life. Between episodes, he came out from behind the camera with an urgent need to tell me, a trusted stranger, his story. Before he was done, I hungered to know more. How had this big burly man survived his own childhood? Who had helped him? When did he get out? What was the source of his hope?

"Charles," I asked, "would you consider writing out your story and sending it to me?"

"That's a new kind of scary thought . . . but, okay—yes. I don't own a computer, but I can get it down on paper for you," he answered.

The writing itself turned out to be one giant step toward freedom. On paper Charles bravely faced the one relationship that had filled his whole life with deep dread. His relentless betrayer wasn't a pedophile, a gang member, an uncle, or the neighborhood bully—but the dangerous woman who'd given birth to him. All he'd ever wanted from her was to feel loved.

To make matters worse, the one man who did love him as a parent should love a child was gone. Daddy wasn't coming back. At the tender age of five, divorce left this young boy in the worst of circumstances—in the custodial care of an unconscionable raging mother. There was no one left at home to intervene on his behalf.

Everyone knows babies are totally defenseless, delightfully innocent, and completely needy. They require lots of attention. Most infants do receive enough love, feel safe, and bond well in trusting relationships with their parents. Unfortunately, there are babies who are deprived of these basic needs. Their start in life is very harsh for one reason—they've had the terrible misfortune to be born to furious mothers.

Charles Rice took his first breath April 5, 1949, at Coronado Naval Air Station, San Diego, California. Both parents were in the Army. He was their only child.

As a toddler he remembers there wasn't much love between his parents. The arguments were continually flying back and forth.

Apart from scripture references, or direct quotes, the words of Charles Rice will appear in italics throughout the book.

EARLY MEMORIES

My mother was almost always the instigator.

I remember the move to Lompoc, California in 1955 where my father was stationed at what was known then as Camp Cook. Today this base is Vandenberg Air Force Base. Not long after the move I noticed something different about my parents.

When bedtime came around, my father began sleeping in another room by himself. Even as a child I thought this was unusual. My parents used to sleep in the same room. I didn't know their behavior meant the family was falling apart. There were many times when I was left in the care of a babysitter while my parents went to something called court.

Over the next few months I knew something was horribly wrong—something I didn't understand. My father took a lot of his stuff with him to work every day. When he came home, the things he had left with that morning weren't with him. My mom and dad had less and less to say to each other except for the big fights between them filled with angry, loud words. The more the words flew back and forth, the madder they would get.

The loud voices made me really afraid. A few times the police even came to the door. The officer would talk to Mom and Dad and things would quiet down for a while.

AN OUTSIDER'S VOICE

An unknown person had overheard the commotion and called the police. That courageous act brought a temporary truce. This is a good reminder that an outsider's voice can make a big difference and prevent the angry party from escalating further.

The fact that Charles's dad started spending even his Sundays on base didn't stop his mother from launching into a one-sided tirade. And the only one within earshot of this toxic verbal abuse was her young son.

She'd rant and rave about how that schmuck, piece of trash, didn't amount to a hill of beans, and was just a total loser. On and on she'd go without end, constantly complaining about him. And he wasn't even there to hear it. Mother would sound so mad that I would get frightened. I would try to go outside, but she'd scream at me to get my ass back inside or I would get the beating of my life.

THE DAY DADDY LEFT

I'll never forget the last time I saw my father. It was on a hot Saturday afternoon. I was playing in the dirt with my toy cars. Daddy stopped at the house long enough to load all the rest of his clothes and things into his car. This took about forty-five minutes. When he was done, he came over to me, knelt down, and started to talk.

"I'm terribly sorry for what's about to happen, Son," he said.

I got scared and asked him what was wrong.

"Your mother and I can no longer get along together," he continued. "I have to leave now and I won't be coming back ever again."

I got this monster-sized scared feeling and began to cry.

My father said he would write to me as often as possible, but I didn't know yet what writing was or what that meant. My mother started to shout at him. "Hurry up and get the hell out of the yard. I'm getting tired of looking at your worthless ass."

Dad tried to hold me close, but Mother yanked me right out of his arms. With contempt in her voice, she spewed, "You've got one minute to leave or I'll call the police."

My father began crying and just kept saying, "I'm sorry; I'm sorry," over and over as he moved toward his car. I remember going after him, arms outstretched, crying harder and louder with each step, and yelling, "Daddy, Daddy, Daddy," over and over. I was *hysterical by the time he started to pull away from the curb. I ran out into the street after him yelling, "DADDY, DADDY . . . COME BACK!"*

TERRIBLY WRONG

Everything about this departing scene screams, "WRONG!" To wait to tell a small child of a change this serious until the moment the parent is leaving is incredibly disrespectful of the child's emotional well-being. Add to that traumatic news the tearing away of the boy from his daddy's arms, and everything Charles knew about feeling safe is now terribly broken.

The parents' messy breakup has brought us face-to-face with a child's first response to abandonment. Fears are real and run deep. Overwhelming sorrow and anguish cannot be missed. Youngsters aren't equipped to understand why a parent chooses to leave. What they do know is the difference between a safe parent and an unsafe parent. Charles is desperately afraid of what his mommy might do to hurt him. Tragically, there's nothing he can do to stop her anger. He's simply too little.

SCARED OUT OF MY WITS

I don't know how far I had run when all of a sudden I was grabbed by my right arm and yanked off my feet so hard it felt like my arm had been broken. Then right there in the street my mother started hitting me on the head, arms, shoulders, and back and kicking me in the backside right there in front of the whole neighborhood. She didn't seem to care if anyone saw her or not. She dragged me by the arm back to the house and into the front room. The minute she turned loose of me, I bolted for the front door to run after my father. My mother caught me at the door and again yanked me as hard as she could by the arm and literally threw me about twenty feet across the huge front room. I came to a stop up against the wall on the other side of the room. I was so afraid! Not only was I crying, I was in total hysterics, as totally scared out of my wits as any little five-year-old boy could be.

The next thing I knew, my mother had come up with one of the biggest belts I had ever seen. It was about four or five inches wide and about as long as her arm, only this belt was folded in half lengthwise and it was still as long as her arm. A sudden white-hot searing pain ripped through my body. Not just once, but over and over and over again, all the while through all this white-hot tearing, burning pain, I seemed to hear my mother just screaming at the top of her lungs, "SHUT UP, SHUT UP, SHUT UP!" Every time she screamed at me, she hit me with that huge belt. Every time she hit me, my body ignited into a paralyzing bolt of white-hot fire from hell. The more she hit me, the more I screamed. All the while, she kept screaming at me to shut up.

A POWER IMBALANCE

This mother was furious! Nothing she did, by any reasonable standards, could be considered appropriate parenting! Rage is a very dangerous companion. If not kept in check, this villain takes over and insists on having her own way.

Those of us who do manage anger appropriately know it's illogical to believe a little kid could stop screaming and crying while being beaten so badly. We also see how heartless it is for any parent to inflict such brutality upon a child. This kind of extreme abuse sometimes leads to death. Consider the huge power imbalance. Young children are at a substantial disadvantage. Their small size and strength make it impossible to fend off a raging parent.

TOO SCARED

Suddenly there was a whole new sensation I hadn't known before. It hurt even worse than what I had been going through. One of her feet flew right at me. I felt this incredible wall of pain sweep over me as she actually kicked me in the ribs! Then she started screaming, "Go to your room, you little bastard! Get out of my sight. I hate you! Get out of my sight before I cut your balls off." I had no clue what that last comment meant, but I skittered off to my room as best I could with Mother right on my heels, still screaming at me, still hitting me with the belt, and still trying to kick me—all at the same time.

I was locked in my room for the rest of the day and all that night. She only let me out once when I cried out that I had to go to the bathroom. Then she locked me right back in my room. No dinner, nothing to drink, nothing!

Sometime the next morning my mother came and opened the door to my room. I was so scared that I dove under my bed. Her voice was calmer, but it was not my mother's voice. There was an eerie guttural, gravelly sound coming from her like one of those voices you hear in monster movies. She sounded controlled but dangerous. "Get out from under the bed," she ordered. "Get to the bathroom."

I was too scared to move. She repeated herself. This time, I moved. I was too scared not to move.

Mother told me to do what I had to do in the toilet. Then she yanked my clothes off and roughly put me in the tub for a five-minute shower. I hurt all over. Every time she touched me it hurt. After my fast shower, I was given a bowl of cold cereal and then locked back in my room for the whole day. That same evening this mean mother came back into my room. I was cringing in a corner as far from the door on the other side of the room as I could get.

The Flashback: Would you believe I'm sitting here crying right now, reliving all of this? It's like I'm watching a video of the whole thing. I can still feel the pain in my body after all these years have gone by.

The Reality: From the day my father left, I lived totally petrified—scared stiff—of my mother. All this time, I just didn't know what I had done to deserve all the pain and bad treatment I was given. I started wondering, in my own little boy way, if I was responsible for what had happened between my father and mother. Nothing this hurtful and terrifying had ever happened to me when they were living together. If only my father was here. Maybe I could run to him for protection from this terrible, horrid, person who had hurt me so badly. Where was my father? Daddy, Daddy, come back home! I'm scared! Mother is hurting me! Come back home and protect me, Daddy! These thoughts kept going through my head day and night. But my daddy, just like he'd told me that day in the yard, didn't ever come home.

DON'T LOSE HOPE

Great portions of this story are painful to read. Some of you might be experiencing flashbacks, too. Please know you were not to blame for the bad things that happened to you. No child ever deserves to be battered.

To look back at undeserved suffering takes courage. One can suppress dark dreadful memories for a while, but it's quite rare to ever forget them. The nature of such intruders is their ability to pop up unexpectedly when triggered by something or someone around you. When that flashback happens, take a minute to recognize its importance. The presence of this unwanted memory is an indication of a deep inner need to resolve a harmful source of tension, dread, or Post-Traumatic Stress Disorder (PTSD). Don't ignore these significant events. Be determined to help these bad memories heal. As these tormentors are brought out into the light, their power over you loses its grip.

Don't lose hope. The fact that you are reading this book may indicate that you are a survivor. If so, God wants to mend those damaged emotions regardless of whether reconciliation takes place with the offender or not. God has made a way for victims of childhood abuse to break free from their past and into the presence of fresh joy.

Understand that God never condones the wrong actions of an atrocious furious parent—not ever! And our Heavenly Father does not want any child to suffer this kind of brutality. But the unwelcome truth is that we live in a fallen world where bad things acted out by calloused, depraved, or mentally ill, people do happen. Innocent children are by far the most unfortunate victims. They are far too small to have any power to stop the abuse or escape its wrath. Often they are deprived the freedom to even shed tears.

If you are ready...

Reach for Fresh Joy *[for the abused]*

> May the God of hope fill you with
> all joy and peace as you trust in him,
> so that you may overflow with hope by the
> power of the Holy Spirit."
> Romans 15:13

> "Be strong and courageous. Do not be afraid
> or terrified because of them,
> for the LORD your God goes with you;
> he will never leave you nor forsake you."
> Deuteronomy 31:6

Begin with a deliberate decision to be courageous. Take a deep breath. Say out loud, "This is now. Today I am no longer the helpless child who could not escape my raging parent. I am a survivor. I am intelligent. I am an adult who has the power to choose not to squander another anxious moment on the woman who didn't protect me, who hurt me so badly."

Fear steps aside when truth is let in. Decide to speak truth *to yourself* until *you* believe what *you* hear. Repeat this positive self-talk throughout the day. Do it again tomorrow and the day after.

How did speaking truth *to yourself* make you feel?
_____
_____
_____
_____

Be courageous. Break your silence. Write out a portion of *your* story:
_____
_____
_____
_____

When you are ready, choose to tell a portion of your story to someone you trust. Who will that person be?
_____
_____
_____
_____

> I sought the Lord, and he answered me;
> he delivered me from all my fears.
> Psalm 34:4

If you are ready...

Reach for Fresh Hope *[for the abuser]*

> But if we hope for what we do not yet have,
> we wait for it patiently.
> Romans 8:25

Take a moment to reflect on your own childhood. Were you abused physically, verbally, or emotionally? _____
Briefly describe what you remember:

_____
_____
_____
_____

How old were you when the abuse began? _____
How did that make you feel?

_____
_____
_____
_____

How old were you when you started abusing others? _____
What triggered that abuse?

_____
_____
_____
_____

Are you ready for a changed life? _____

Are you ready to learn how to love and nurture in godly ways? _____

If so, the best place to begin is to admit the wrongs and have a genuine repentant heart. Ask the Lord and your children to forgive you. There is good in you, but you must tap into its presence. God put good in you.

Say out loud, "Today I am an adult who has the power to choose good behaviors over destructive ones. I am ready to become the caring person God intends me to be, but on my own I am not strong enough. Lord, help me to change. Teach me self-control. I don't like me when I am abusive to my children. They deserve better. Free me from this darkness, I pray."

Speak truth *to yourself* until *you* believe what *you* hear. Repeat this positive talk throughout the day. Do it again tomorrow and the day after.

How did speaking truth *to yourself* and asking for God's help make you feel?

_____
_____

> How can I know all the sins lurking in my heart?
> Cleanse me from these hidden faults.
> Psalm 19:12 NLT

Home is the one place in all this world where hearts are sure of each other. It is the place of confidence. It is the place where we tear off that mask of guarded and suspicious coldness which the world forces us to wear in self-defense, and where we pour out the unreserved communications of full and confiding hearts. It is the spot where expressions of tenderness gush out without any sensation of awkwardness and without any dread of ridicule.

— Frederick W. Robertson

TWO

"Mommy, Where's Daddy?"

Two days after my father left, my mother finally let me out of my room. I sat at the dining table and had more cold cereal and orange juice to drink. Just as I was finishing my breakfast, drinking the last of my orange juice, I asked, "Mommy, where's Daddy?"

Suddenly she lunged across the table and hit me with her fist right in the side of my face. I went flying out of my chair and landed across the room—about fifteen feet away. My whole head felt like it had just been blown up. I had blood coming out of my mouth where what few teeth I had, had deeply cut the inside of my cheek. Mother flew out of her chair, came up to me and proceeded to kick me just as hard as she could right in my testicles. That was the last thing I remembered. Everything went black after the explosion of pain that resulted from her kick. I didn't know it then, but I had passed out.

AN INNOCENT QUESTION

Out of control doesn't begin to describe this enraged mother's actions. For those of you who are, or have been, on the receiving end of such vicious child abuse, questions like this one are innocent, reasonable, to be expected, and deserve a gentle answer—not a ruthless beating!

Realize all small children enter a "Why?" stage and are full of questions. It is natural for Daddy's whereabouts to be on your mind. Your sense of security was shaken. There is nothing wrong about missing someone you love and rightly wanting to hear something that would make sense and quiet your fears.

ABUSERS—DON'T PRACTICE PARENT ALIENATION

Lots of families experience divorce. Mine did, too, when I was sixteen. But the family breaking apart should not mean war erupts between parents or that innocent little ones, who didn't want the family to split up, are caught in the crossfire.

Parents, for the good of the children, get beyond the personal agenda. The marriage is over, but the child still has two parents. Find ways to be respectful to that ex—not loathsome. Learn to embrace the new reality of co-parenting with maturity. Don't inflict unnecessary emotional damage on the children. Give them a positive childhood experience.

When one parent alienates the other, the child is caught in a trap of divided loyalties. Don't damage your child's heart by alienating the parent. Instead, be sensitive. Keep personal emotions in check in order to reassure your child that they will be okay, that Daddy and Mommy still loves him/her even though he won't live with them anymore.

ADVOCATE FOR AT-RISK CHILDREN

Those who have been victims of abuse are 1,000 times more likely to become abusers themselves. If that describes you, or you are acquainted with an abuser, please become part of the solution. Reach out to stop the cycle of abuse. Get help for yourself or find the words to encourage another person to hunt down needed changes. Several resources are included at the end of this book.

Furious mothers have a very short and selfish fuse. In a split second, rage dominates whatever happens next. This could easily be an outpouring of their own upbringing, but this behavior negatively affects the children. Youngsters get hurt when mommy-anger runs wild. At-risk children have no choice but to learn early what it means to live in an unstable, unsafe, world where there is no way of escape. Their reality doesn't include a loving bond between a mother and child. This pattern, because it's laid down at such an early age, has the power to mold individuals for a lifetime of relationship insecurities.

Bad parenting does not have to continue, nor should it be silently allowed to persist. Dare to speak up. Risk not being liked if it means keeping a child safe. Sometimes all it takes is a verbal push to move an abuser in the direction of help. The payoff could be a better, safer, happier, childhood for one of the young innocents who today cowers in the presence of an all-out seething rage-aholic.

Advocates play an important role. Children like Charles Rice are too little to defend themselves and have nowhere to hide. Unless someone speaks up, the innocence of childhood is lost all too soon. A parent who continues to act out with wild fits of rage teaches a child that it's not safe to speak their thoughts out loud. How could little Charles have known his simple question at breakfast would become the biggest mistake of his entire day? Instead of a kind answer, he became the victim of outrageous contemptible abuse.

MACARONI AND CHEESE

Much later I woke up on the couch in the front room and the sun was shining in the window, so I knew it was sometime in the afternoon. My mother was laughing and joking with someone on the phone. The last thing she said, to whoever it was, was that she would be home all day so this person could come over whenever they wanted, and then she hung up.

A little while later the doorbell rang and just before my mother answered the door, she threateningly told me to go to my room and not to come out until she told me I could. I made a beeline for my room. Just as I got to the door of my room, I heard a man's deep-pitched voice.

I stayed in my room and started playing with my toys and, in a little while, I started hearing all kinds of strange noises coming from under my door. I crept over and quietly opened my door just a little to try and see what the strange groaning noises were. At this point, do I have to say what all those moaning and groaning and grunting noises were? Remember I was just five years old. I didn't know what it was. So I just sneaked back to my room and very quietly closed my door after seeing into my mother's room through the open door.

Little kids have no idea of time passage, but it seemed like forever before she came into my room and said I could go play outside. As I went out the door, I saw the guy was gone.

That evening my dinner consisted of sauerkraut, beets, macaroni and cheese, a bologna sandwich and a glass of water. Then back to my room for the night. My mother came in and told me when to go to bed. She turned out the light and reclosed the door.

The next day, she opened my door and told me to get into the bathroom and do what I had to do and get ready for a shower. Once everything was done, she got me dressed and there was a babysitter there to take care of me for the day while she went to work.

That is how the week would go until the weekends. That was when it didn't take much for her to flip out and take out her rage against me. I began to dread and even hate weekends because Saturday and Sunday was when I was in the most danger of being beaten, kicked, deprived of food, locked in my room, and anything else her weird mind could conceive.

I was never allowed to have any friends because, as my mother would say, "I don't want a whole bunch of noisy, hell-raising brats around this house." So guess who didn't get to mix with all the other kids my age in the neighborhood?

VIVID DETAILS

Notice the details. They are so vivid. All these years later, the plate of food he was given decades ago remains crystal clear, as if a snapshot were framed. Fear is a great heightener of awareness. Charles was all ears, not wanting Mother to get mad at him again. He focused on his own safety, down to the macaroni and beets on the plate.

Let's not forget that Charles's mother was a competent woman, skilled at doing her day job in an acceptable manner. And yet, the woman she was in the presence of her peers was very different from the mother she was at home. This pattern seems to indicate she *could* make good decisions, *could* be mindful of controlling her temper when it was advantageous to do so, but she did not carry the same considerate thought processes into parenting her son.

Whenever two inconsistent codes of conduct are uncovered, the Bible labels this condition as "double-minded" (James 1:8; 4:8). The public face looks good to the outside world, but the private face is far from good-natured. At home this mother was rude, bad-tempered, and utterly frightening. All decency stopped at the front door. From what Charles has told of his childhood, the sufferings he endured, there was no indication that his bully mom believed she was doing wrong—or that she should change.

ISOLATED

To isolate a child from other children is not natural or nice. In abusive homes, this serves only one purpose; it's to assure the dirty secrets, those cruel things taking place behind closed doors, stay hidden from outsiders.

Childhood friends are important. Playing with neighboring boys and girls is one of the best parts of growing up. When this interaction isn't happening, red flags should fly. Apart from a rare medical condition or unusual safety concern (both highly uncommon), isolating a child from peer interaction smells of deliberate parental abuse. A common technique of an abuser is to isolate the targeted individual. In doing so, limited exposure to what is happening inside the home can be achieved. Strangely, they believe their shameful behaviors won't be discovered. Too often they are right.

OUTSIDERS CAN HELP

What can outsiders do? Plenty! If we know a family has children and do not routinely see those children, we could be concerned enough to knock on their door in a neighborly way. A plate of cookies might be welcomed and make the knocking less awkward. If there's a gnawing sense that something is wrong, make a phone call. Ask authorities to investigate. Cases have been in the news where children have been kept out of sight—sometimes for years. And, if there are loud noises, lots of arguing or screaming beyond the typical family spat, choose to stand in the gap—to blow the whistle before a tragedy happens.

There are multiple places where abuse can be reported and help found. Some are listed in the resources chapter at the end of this book.

MISUNDERSTOOD

In school I was always standoffish and quiet. Even during things like recess and P.E. and other school-time activities, I was always the one who stayed off to one side. As I got older, this habit didn't change. Other things started to happen that added more problems to my life at home and at school.

The time came when I was required to participate in many other school activities. Guess who flat refused to take part in these activities? When the weather was bad, we didn't go outside to have recess. Instead, we all had to go to the gymnasium to take part in things like dodgeball. This is where certain kids line up against a wall and let other kids throw big balls at them. And, of course, there are always a few school bully types who get great sadistic delight out of throwing those balls at you just as hard as they can, hoping they will hurt you. These bully types did things like this for many reasons. Maybe they didn't like you. Maybe they thought you were "weird." Maybe they thought you were a sissy or a coward, or they would take out their bad attitude on you just to be a bully and make all the other kids scared of them, too.

Most people can remember some sort of run-in with these bully types over the course of their school years. Bullies didn't need any reason at all to find someone to pick on or to beat up. So when these indoor activities had to take place, once again guess who always headed for the nearest door?

Why stand there like a total idiot and let some sadistic bully throw something at you with the express intent of hurting you? That's really kind of stupid, and even at the age of six, seven, or eight, it didn't take much reasoning of any kind to realize that someone was trying to hurt me, and I would run away from that threat. When I ran from the gym, the stupid teachers would run after me and force me back into the gym, where I would again run at the first opportunity. I would eventually be sent to the principal's office.

Then the obvious would take place. The principal would ask me why I would not take part in activities. I would answer in short clipped sentences like, "Don't like it" or "Afraid." The principal would ask, "Afraid of what?" to which I'd answer, "Afraid of being hurt. Don't like being hurt." These principals NEVER seemed to understand what I meant. They'd always end up threatening me that if I didn't start participating in these activities, I'd be kept after school. That would scare me to death, because I knew from other past experiences of the same kind that if I was kept after school for ANY reason, I'd get the beating of my life when I got home.

LABELED NONCOMPLIANT

If things weren't already bad enough, the school added to the problem. This portion of Charles's story reveals a very fearful, distraught child. Saying he was "afraid of being hurt" should have rung out like a fire alarm in the principal's ears. But it didn't back then. What a difference it could have made in this boy's life if his fears had been taken seriously. His reasons for not wanting to play ball made perfect sense. Labeling noncompliant behaviors as disobedience or nonconformity to classroom rules did nothing to protect him from fear of physical harm. Quite the opposite was true.

Hindsight is available now. Better solutions could have been brought to the table. Teachers, the coach, and the principal might have asked the boy to participate at a different level—like ball gatherer or scorekeeper. Children like Charles desperately need to be empowered to succeed, especially if that means opting out of a class in order to feel safe.

More punishment was the last thing this boy needed. He

was being truthful. The answers he gave deserved to be taken seriously. "Afraid" was raw honesty. Under the circumstances, he had dropped big clues about what was happening off school grounds. Had someone looked deeper into the matter, Charles's childhood might have turned out differently.

Instead, knowing his mean mother would be told of his lack of cooperation only heightened his fears. He knew, beyond any doubt, that going home on those days would mean danger awaited him.

The coach verbally bullied this student. To be fair, let's cut the principal a little slack. From Charles's own words, the man did not know the brutality taking place in his home nor the bruises concealed under his clothing. How could he have understood that the boy he'd spoken with earlier that day, the one he'd tried to talk into being compliant, would be viciously beaten by his mother before the day was over? Almost certainly, this principal would have acted differently had he known about the beatings.

If you are ready...2

Reach for Fresh Joy *[for the abused]*

"Ask and you will receive, and your joy will be complete."
John 16:24

Allow time to mourn the absence of a happy childhood. Validate those feelings. The pain you endured was real. Those life-wounds hurt. But don't allow yourself to get stuck in that sad and lonely place. That's not God's good plan for you. Move on by gathering grief management skills through books or therapy sessions. Some suggestions are given in the Addendum: Resources at the end of the book. The right resources will point you to a path of forgiveness for people, like the school principal, who likely didn't know about the abuse happening at your house and inadvertently caused you more harm.

Who, lacking clarity of your home circumstances at the time, added to your troubles?

_____
_____
_____

What authority did this person hold over you?

_____
_____
_____

Were there others who put you in danger?
_____
_____
_____

Who? _____

How much truth about your home life were these individuals privy to?
_____
_____
_____
_____
_____

Begin to free yourself from the dark memories. Take the next bold step. As you are able, choose to forgive these individuals. This single unpretentious act will bless you ten thousand times over and lines up with God's will for His children.

Pray a simple prayer like this one: "Lord, You've forgiven me so much. I am so thankful. Please forgive me for harboring unforgiveness toward _____, _____, and _____ (Name as many as you need to.) Please take the bitterness from me. Purge it from my heart and my mind. I'm tired of such filth manipulating my life. Fill me with a heaping measure of Your joy. Amen."

David's Prayer: The Bible calls David a man after God's own heart. And yet he was a hunted man. King Saul wanted him dead. While hiding in a cave, David prays a prayer, found in Psalm 142:2–7, that shows us how to cry out to the Lord when life is full of troubles and we feel desperate.

> "I pour out before him my complaint; before him I tell my trouble. When my spirit grows faint within me, it is you who watch over my way. In the path where I walk people have hidden a snare for me. Look and see, there is no one at my right hand; no one is concerned for me. I have no refuge; no one cares for my life. I cry to you, LORD; I say, You are my refuge, my portion in the land of the living." Listen to my cry, for I am in desperate need; rescue me from those who pursue me, for they are too strong for me. Set me free from my prison, that I may praise your name. Then the righteous will gather about me because of your goodness to me."

How does David's prayer meet your heart's need?

_____
_____
_____

If you are ready...

Reach for Fresh Hope *[for the abuser]*

"All of you, clothe yourselves with humility
toward one another, because,
'God opposes the proud but shows favor
to the humble.'"
1 Peter 5:5

Outrageous anger scares children. Be honest with yourself as you name things you have done that frightened your children:
_____
_____
_____
_____

What might have triggered you to lash out at your children?
_____
_____
_____
_____

What is your greatest regret?
_____
_____
_____
_____

> "Human anger does not produce the
> righteousness that God desires." James 1:20

You are created in God's image. Let that thought sink deep into your being. God's kids are capable of living righteous lives. What would living righteously look like for you?

_____

_____

_____

_____

> "Who is wise and understanding among you?
> Let them show it by their good life,
> by deeds done in the humility
> that comes from wisdom."
> James 3:13

Self-image and self-esteem are the most powerful forces affecting how we deal with anger. When we don't feel good about ourselves, when our self-esteem is low, then we are more prone to act in anger. When we perceive ourselves accurately, when our self-image is correct and we recognize that we are valuable and worthy of love, then we can cope with the inevitable temptations to react in anger.[3]

— Kathy Collard Miller

THREE
ALL HELL EXPLODED AROUND ME

As a little kid I never knew or understood why my mother would fly into these totally unbelievable fits of blind rage. What I understood clearly was that when this happened, I was the one who caught the end result of her rage.

As I got a little older, around eleven and twelve years old, the next trick my mother came up with was to check my room while I was at school. If my room wasn't next to hospital operating room clean, she'd sweep through and toss everything off the shelves onto the floor. The same was true for the closet and the dresser. I'd come home from school and be met at the front door by the belt and the bad attitude from hell.

The belt would fly as soon as I opened the door. I wouldn't even see it coming or even know what I was getting whipped for. Then my mother would start screaming at me that my room was a filthy pigsty and I should get my useless lazy ass in there and clean my room. As I'd head for my room, guess who was right behind me swinging that belt like a bullwhip?

Once in my room, I saw it looked like the aftermath of Hurricane Josephine. Oh, by the way, my mother's first name is Josephine. Even the blankets were ripped off the bed and thrown on the floor. It was like trying to clean up New Orleans after Hurricane Katrina, while being hotly pursued by the ever-swinging belt.

My dear sweet mother [sarcasm intended] made me take out the garbage, even if there was just one tuna or soup can in the bottom of the kitchen garbage bucket. If I tried to ask why I had to take out the garbage when it was clear there was none to take out, she'd backhand me in the face as hard as she could, and scream at me, "BECAUSE I TOLD YOU TO, THAT'S WHY!"

I never did understand why she always screamed at the top of her lungs at me. She hardly ever spoke in a calm, normal volume or tone. Maybe that's how she got her jollies—by being loud, overbearing, dominant, controlling, and authoritative. As an eleven or twelve-year-old, I couldn't help but wonder if she talked like that to her coworkers. Did she fly into a rage if something went wrong at work, too?

WANDERING INTO TROUBLE

Many were the days I was alone in the house with specific orders not to go outside for any reason. I look back on that remark and suppose that meant that even if the house was on fire, I was not to go outside for any reason; just burn up with the house.

On some of the occasions when my mother was gone for hours on end, yes, you guessed it; I'd go outside. I'd wander the neighborhood and eventually, like all kids who have nothing to do but hang out, I got into trouble. It wasn't too bad, but it was *enough to get my mother called down to the local police station to bring me home. You can guess what happened when she found out that I had tried to break into a music shop. I never got into the shop because the owner was inside, doing something and heard me at the back door. Next thing I knew, I had the store owner in front of me holding one of the biggest guns I had ever seen.*

I can say that I wasn't really trying to break into that shop to steal anything, I was just a stupid kid, out all alone just messing around and one thing led to another. I was just trying something I had never done before. Maybe I was looking for attention; maybe that was my own confused plea for help. I don't know. You can imagine the hurricane I encountered when I got home. Mother made me wish that I was dead or worse. Or both! As far as the cops were concerned, it was a matter soon forgotten altogether. This did start my juvenile police record, but I never got in any other trouble with the police as a juvenile.

EXTREME PUNISHMENT IS NEVER CONSTRUCTIVE DISCIPLINE

After reading Charles's words, take a moment to breathe. To say his mother was out of control is more than a gross misstatement. She's as wild as the strongest of hurricanes. The behaviors were premeditated. She laid in wait, brewed up destruction, watched the front door for the perfect opportunity to unleash pent-up hostility and inflict pain. While we do not know the payoff she was looking for (and there had to be some twisted gratification gained), we can categorize this parenting style as depraved, heartless, and brutal.

Constructive discipline cannot be effectively carried out through destructive means. Tearing apart a room in a wild rage doesn't teach a child how to responsibly care for his room. To the contrary, it enrages the child. Nor does beating a child within an inch of his life come anywhere near the realm of appropriate discipline.

Charles Rice endured intense inexcusable abuse. There is no indication that his mother wanted to control her anger toward him. Quite the opposite. She was bent on beating the tar out of her son time after time. We might assume her goal was to literally "whip" him into shape. Again, that kind of thinking is completely unacceptable, injurious, and far from good discipline.

Extreme punishment toward a child is not discipline! It is ruthless cruelty that could land a child in the hospital—or worse—and a parent behind bars. Not sometimes . . . but at all times.

APPROPRIATE DISCIPLINE

What is godly discipline? "Disciple" is the root word of "discipline." Jesus was a disciple-maker. He taught by example what it means to teach, or *disciple*, those under our authority. The teacher, or parent, is to see the recipient (in this case the child) as an apprentice to tutor and inspire toward excellence. The teacher recognizes the importance of leading by example to illustrate what is expected of her young disciple.

Disciple-makers understand that when correction is needed (and it will be), the right way to change a behavior is to confront in love—never to give in to furious or explosive actions. As frustrating as the moment might be, think first. Remember to model love in the midst of discipline. Appropriate consequences are often necessary to the process, but no physical or emotional harm should be done to the apprentice.

Let's revisit Charles's torn-apart bedroom. What could have been done differently? Just about everything.

- Rather than making his room worse, a disciple-making mom sees the messy room as an opportunity to teach basic tidying up skills.

- She uses a calm voice to make her point.

- She trains him how to pick up toys, hang up clothes, dust shelves, and make his bed.

- Her interaction with the child is age appropriate and makes use of respectful language while explaining what is expected.

- The disciple-making parent has hangers available, shelves for books, and storage bins for toys and shows the child how to use the vacuum cleaner and bag up the trash.

- She comes alongside her son and offers to help the first couple of times.

- Age-appropriate consequences back up what is being taught and are clearly explained upfront.

Each step is one of positive reinforcement and of leading by example. The next time the room is looking shabby, the mom mentions what needs to be done and reminds him of the consequences. If the problem is not corrected, the consequences fall into place. There won't be ice cream tonight, or a favorite television show, or time with a friend, or screen time on the computer. Again, no physical or emotional harm is done.

When parenting and discipline are appropriate, there's no need to scream, fly into a rage, or spew insults. Simply be consistent and let the consequences do the teaching. This kind of discipline brings about the desired objective with the least amount of drama. The child is unharmed and not enraged. Parents are rewarded as disciple-style parenting causes children to develop respect for authority over time.

JESUS LOVES CHILDREN

Children are special to the Lord. Never doubt that Jesus loves children. His words in Matthew 18:3–6 might surprise you:

> "Truly I tell you, unless you change and become like little children, you will never enter the kingdom of heaven. Therefore, whoever takes the lowly position of this child is the greatest in the kingdom of heaven. And whoever welcomes one such child in my name welcomes me. If anyone causes one of these little ones— who believe in me—to stumble, it would be better for them to have a large millstone hung around their neck and to be drowned in the depths of the sea."

Are you surprised to learn all of us who say we love the Lord must come to Him as a little child? An interesting thought to ponder. A child-like simple trust is a prerequisite for every Christ-follower.

Let the emphasis Jesus places on the importance of children sink in as an incentive to parent well or suffer serious consequences. These words are also suitable for anyone (teachers, coaches, youth leaders, extended family) who holds authority or influence over a young person's life. Take that role seriously. Train carefully. God, who loves children, is watching. Remember you are helping to shape a child's future.

THE DOWNSIDE OF SAYING "NO"

When I started into the seventh grade, a completely new campaign of assault on me took place by my mother. We were living in Dunsmuir, California. Dunsmuir Elementary had a policy that everyone dress down to gym shorts and t-shirt for P.E. class. Well guess who absolutely would NOT dress down for P.E.? Me. And for very good reasons.

No young teen with great big black and blue welts from belt beatings and big angry bruises on them from being kicked is going to dress down and be embarrassed to death or made fun of by the other students. NO WAY JOSÉ! My lack of cooperation meant phase two would kick in. The coach would get on my case for not dressing down. He'd get real macho and get right down physically in my face and start with his holier-than-thou-moron diatribe.

"What's the matter with you, your lordship? Are you an exception to the rules around here? Are you too royal to dress down?" And all other kinds of really stupid insults.

I'd just stand there and get defiant and raise my voice and tell him I wasn't dressing down, and if he didn't like it . . . I think you know what I said. Well, that started another avalanche in motion. I'd get sent to the principal's office, and the whole thing would start going around and around again, like a merry-go-round. The principal would ask me why I wouldn't dress down for P.E. I'd just tell him I wasn't going to dress down. End of story. Period!

You see back in the 50s and 60s, whether you were a kid or an adult, things like this just were not discussed, period. It was taboo! So I sulked in the principal's office and would not give him an answer. In the beginning, I got hit with detention, time after time. Every time this happened, of course, my dear mother knew about it because I'd come in the door late. I'd get grilled as to why I was late. I'd tell her why. She'd then order me to dress down for P.E. and I'd tell her, "No, I will not dress down. I will not be made fun of by all the other kids when they see all the welts and bruises you put on me."

That only made matters worse. Then she'd threaten me that if I didn't start doing what I was supposed to do at school, she would beat me until I was senseless.

So the next day, back to school I'd go and, come P.E. time, guess what? Here we'd go again, the browbeating from the coach, the trip to the principal's office, but now a new twist. I got suspended! I got suspended sometimes on a weekly basis just because I wouldn't dress down for P.E. See how things just kept getting worse and worse and worse? I didn't have to do anything at all, and all hell would literally explode around me.

The first two or three times I got suspended, I was able to figure a way around it that my mother wouldn't find out about. But that only worked the first two or three times. Then the dumb school pulled their new rabbit out of the hat. The fools sent letters to my mother telling her what was going on.

Well, I guess you know by now that when I walked in the door, I walked into Mt. Krakatoa in full explosion stage: the screaming in fury, the flying belt, the scream of pain, the confinement to my room for the remainder of the day, the going to bed without meals, being grounded all weekend long. It just went on and on and so I'd just sit in my room and sulk and even hide in my closet with the door closed for hours.

One day one of these incidents turned really explosive when I tried to stand up against my mother. She flew into a rage that would have scared King Kong, Godzilla, and God. The belt began to fly and I don't know if it was an accident or not, but the belt buckle came out of her hand as she was beating me for sassing her, and the buckle hit me in the head and laid my forehead open. She rushed me to the hospital and it took three stitches to close up the cut. But to this day that crescent scar can still be seen in the edge of my hairline on my left forehead. I also have two or three other scars on me from my dear mother that I will carry to my grave.

It didn't take long for my teenage smarts to realize that if I didn't stay home too much, I couldn't be beaten as often. I was a thirteen-year-old with a bicycle. I'd go out riding my bike as much as possible. Then one day I got kind of lucky; I landed a paper route. In the beginning, the paper route was small, but within a year I delivered more than 500 papers every afternoon after school. That helped keep me away from the house for a couple of extra hours. Oh, don't get me wrong. It didn't stop my mother any. It just slowed her up a little. When I was home, I still caught all kinds of flak for just about anything you can imagine.

A CODE OF SILENCE

Adolescence was a terrible time for Charles Rice. Saying "No" was never respected. Not at school, and certainly not at home. This boy was repetitively beat up verbally, physically, and emotionally. Since he refused to reveal why he wouldn't comply, there was nowhere for him to turn for help. Instead, he held tightly to a code of silence.

Today, child advocacy centers can be found in most communities. There are court-appointed child advocates to help a child get out of harmful situations. If someone dares to come forward, and risks butting in, abuse can be stopped. Todays teachers are trained in proper disciplinary actions and how to spot abuse. By law they have to report those concerns to the proper authorities.

Sadly, not every incident is discovered. Hundreds of thousands of boys and girls are still living in homes where there is an unsafe, furious parent. Like Charles, these boys and girls are bound by a web of secrecy and fear of telling.

BECOMING CREATIVE

A lot of credit goes to Charles for becoming a resourceful kid. Most definitely he proved himself a survivor. Figuring out how to avoid being home more than was absolutely necessary was smart. That daily paper route provided a valid reason to be away from home each day and supplied spending money.

An intense need to survive a dangerous situation often cultivates creativity and ignites independent thinking.

If you are ready...

Reach for Fresh Joy *[for the abused]*

> "In all these things we are more
> than conquerors through him who loved us."
> Romans 8:37

God calls you a conqueror! You've stared down trouble and, despite the scars, come out on top. Never forget you are God's child, treasured and dearly loved. God has wired you with a deep hunger to survive. That's a good thing. One way to recognize that you are strong is to look in a mirror. After all you've gone through, you are still here. Those blows did not take you out! Why? The best reason to arrive at is that God has a purpose for your life. Believe that in Him lies your victory and purpose. The future is bright.

As a survivor, name some of the painful things you managed to live through:

_____
_____
_____

How do you think you prevailed over such awful, inexcusable, and cruel parenting?

_____
_____
_____

Pinpoint a few behaviors that served you well (determination, daring, anger, silence, honesty, dishonesty, caution, suspicious, guardedness, shrewdness, restraint, compliance, etc.):

_____
_____
_____
_____

Describe how those actions helped to keep you safe:

_____
_____
_____
_____

Single out a few behaviors that brought you more trouble (speaking up, stubbornness, boldness, caution, anger, boasting, laziness, kindness, fearfulness, honesty, dishonesty, running away, etc.):

_____
_____
_____
_____

Describe how those actions worked against you:

_____
_____
_____
_____

Thank Jesus for the bravery and strength you possess. Those are beautiful gifts from above. Receive and believe the promise found in Romans 8:37: You are a conqueror. God says so! Tuck this courage-filled verse into the depths of your heart. Let it permeate every fiber of your being. Consider writing out Romans 8:37 on a notecard or whiteboard. Put it in several visible places: at home, in your car, or at work. Never forget this bold promise from God.

If you are ready...

Reach for Fresh Hope *[for the abuser]*

> "Let your conversation be always full of grace,
> seasoned with salt, so that you may know
> how to answer everyone."
> Colossians 4:6

Describe a typical conversation you would have with your child. What is your tone and choice of words?

_____
_____
_____
_____
_____
_____

How has your child reacted to those talks? ____ fearful ____ angry ____ tears ____ silence ____ cooperative ____ other (describe)

_____
_____
_____
_____

Were you the recipient of filthy language as a child? _____
How did that make you feel?

_____
_____
_____
_____

Were you physically beaten as a child? _____
What were your thoughts toward that parent?

_____
_____
_____
_____

In your mind, trade places with your child. What effect do you think your words and/or beatings have had on his/her life?

_____
_____
_____
_____

What difference might it make if your speech was sprinkled with grace instead of malice?

_____
_____
_____
_____
_____

"I can do all things through him who gives me strength."
Philippians 4:13

It is a wisdom that has faced the pain caused by parents, spouse, family, friends, colleagues, business associates, and has truly forgiven them and acknowledged with unexpected compassion that these people are neither angels nor devils, but only human.[4]

— Brennan Manning

FOUR

THE LAST TWO YEARS OF HIGH SCHOOL

My last two years of high school were spent at Fortuna High in Rio Dell, in California's beautiful Humboldt County. I also worked nights and sometimes weekends at Pacific Lumber Company in Scotia, California. As the years came and went, my mother got worse. During that time I was the only one bringing in money. That meant I had other responsibilities laid on me.

I worked on the mill's "A" dry sorter, pulling chain, for what was then known as contract wages. It was not too unusual for all of us on that chain to make $1,800 to $2,200 every two weeks. We worked our hearts out. Personally, I absolutely loved the job. Here I was just seventeen years old and making good money. I had good friends to work with and also a way to release all my pent-up frustrations and aggressions by pouring it all into pulling lumber.

By now, I also had my first car. So when weekends came around, maximum effort went into getting "lost" (without my mother's knowledge). Being away from home on weekends with a small bunch of friends from school was the safest place to be. We *never hit the same beach twice. The getaways were spread out up and down the northern California coastline between Shelter Cove and Crescent City to lessen our chance of being found. Only Mary's parents knew our whereabouts.*

Yeah, you guessed it. Girls, booze, pot, the open beach, wind in your face, sand under your feet, nights under starry skies, campfires, and the sound of the surf. It was all intoxicating. A warm soft female against you; yeah, things happened. This was a whole new world for me. I had never known this kind of freedom before.

The only way I was able to get this freedom was to outthink, outfox, my mother. But there were times when the secret place didn't work. And as you can already figure out, the fireworks factory exploded in my face.

During those last couple of years of high school, my mother was taking college courses at Redwood College at the south end of Eureka, five days a week from 8 a.m. until nearly 6 p.m. She was working toward a teaching degree. (God help the students she might have.) As I said before, I was the only one bringing in any money at that time. I paid the rent, lights, telephone, gas, and other household expenses every month, including gas in my car and my mother's car. As such, I felt I was in a position to demand my own way to a certain extent and my mother knew immediately that I indeed held the upper hand. But sometimes even the upper hand didn't save me.

All through high school I had a hobby of collecting records. Remember records . . . those discs made of vinyl or shellac played on a record player? Today, there are people who really and truly do not know what a record is. But in the late 60s, while 45s were the record of choice, there were still lots of old 78-rpm records available, and I had a big collection of 78s. Especially the ones on the Sun Records label with admired artists like Elvis Presley, Carl Perkins, Johnny Cash, and other rock-a-billy artists. I also had 78s by Caruso, Mario Lanza, Tommy Dorsey, Bill Haley, Little Richard, Cowboy Copas, and many others. My prized collection had a wide variety of music.

One Friday morning, I had gassed up both my car and my mom's so she could get to school that Friday and I could get to school and to work after school. What she didn't know was that during lunch at school, I made a fast dash home and got a bunch of food, clothes, my sleeping bag, and other things. I loaded them into the car and headed back to school. After school, I dropped off some of the stuff at my girlfriend's house. Boy, oh boy, was my mother totally ticked off about me having a girlfriend. I then headed back to the house to get just a couple of other things before heading to work.

What my mother didn't know was that I intended to go straight from work to get my girlfriend and the stuff I had dropped off, and head for the South Jetty where our friends were waiting for us. Everything went according to plan and I stayed gone until Sunday. I rolled in my driveway about 3 p.m. Twilight was coming on. The driveway was empty. The house was dark.

A FEELING OF DREAD

A feeling of dread floated down over me. I quietly let myself in and turned on the kitchen light. Okay—so far, so good. I went to the front room and turned on a light. Okay again. I went out to get some of my stuff from the car and headed to my room. With one free finger, I flipped on the light. My room looked like the Murrah

Federal Building after it had been bombed. Not one thing was where it belonged.

My bed was flipped upside down, the closet stripped and everything thrown on the floor. My total record collection of about 2,000 records was thrown and broken all over the room, Records, worth five times their original price on the collector market today, laid in broken fragments by the thousands.

Comic books of Superman, Batman, and The Green Lantern were torn and shredded in confetti-sized pieces all over the room. I was devastated. I felt so violated. Anger rose up in me. At that moment, if my mother had been home, I might have been capable of killing her.

I flew into my own black rage. How could she do something like this to my possessions? How dare she invade the privacy of my room! What the hell was her problem?

THE NATURE OF ABUSE IS TO ESCALATE

Those who are being abused need to know that the nature of abuse is to escalate. Each incident has the potential to become more dangerous than the last one. And the abuser cannot begin to stop abusing until she/he understands this truth, too, and wants to get help.

For Charles Rice, the pattern of abuse continued to escalate. Now we've learned of a full-blown spiteful attack on his personal property. His mother abuser went after anything she knew was prized by her son.

Oh, how I wish this could be fiction, just a bad dream soon to be awakened from, instead of a real-life tragedy. Without the son to smash around, the abuser was still bent on venting her rage and sought to destroy what he held dear.

Do you remember what was said about a mother's influence? Charles's mother was a prime example of a toxic, unpredictable, dangerous parent whose influence scores a negative 10 times ten on a scale of 1 to10. Since children are prone to pick up a parent's habits, Charles was groomed, consciously or subconsciously, to also fly into a rage. He's man-sized now, ready to graduate from high school, holding a man's job as a millworker, and physically stronger than before. But his emotional maturity to process life's problems successfully is lacking, limited by the parenting example he was exposed to in his formative years.

If I were to take a poll, 99.9% of us would agree that Charles's anger is justified. What has happened to him angers me. Anger serves a good purpose *only* if it leads to solutions and not to sin. Righteous anger pushes us to make needed changes. But boiling-over rage is a wild beast incapable of solving any problem in an appropriate way. Rage freaks people out, stirs up more anger in others, spews verbal carnage, has the potential to inflict physical harm (or death), is totally self-serving, and is out-and-out abusive and insulting.

Nothing good ever came from this mother's raging heartless behaviors. She continued to batter her child emotionally, verbally, and physically. When Charles asked, "What's her problem?" he was onto something that needed answering. There is no doubt that the cause of his mother's injurious behaviors should have been dealt with years earlier.

A great number of furious mothers don't like how they parent. They are ashamed, and even want to stop, but they don't take the time to figure out how to live in the throes of life's day-to-day frustrating stuff without escalating to a full-blown rage.

ANGER WITHOUT SIN

Anger can be expressed without sin once there is an understanding of what anger really is. Anger is always the secondary emotion—an immediate reaction to what is happening. Anger is used to cover up the real emotion that needs attention. That's the level we need to get down to, to recognize, validate, and work through.

A whole host of fears and insecurities sleep beneath the surface. If we want to stop anger's sinful cycle and stop vomiting hurt onto others, we'll need to look into our deepest fears and insecurities. What do we fear? Rejection or being hurt? Abandonment or loss of security? Is embarrassment our problem? Or is our reputation threatened?

When we dare to confront those personal rascals, old fears fall away. Humility and confidence find room to emerge. Old behaviors can now give way to God-centered solutions.

Every one of us struggles with anger. Those who've been abused are rightfully angry. But that temperament should not be allowed to hold us hostage. Successful anger management depends on good communication skills. There are many ways to gather these skills.

1. Read a book
2. Take a class
3. Join a support group
4. Talk with a counselor or a life coach
5. Learn to set healthy boundaries

Above all, do *something*! Anger can be expressed in good ways.

Recognizing what healthy boundaries look like is another way to tap into our authentic selves. This will require us to discover our core values. From those values we determine in advance how we will allow others to treat us. This step will help us to know what to do when our boundaries are crossed and we are not treated with dignity and respect. For instance, if words turn to yelling, we might choose to go for a walk to lessen the tension.

The day we choose not to allow our emotional well-being to suffer under the weight of abuse is the day life can begin to change for the better. Good relationships take work, but they will only improve if we learn to set healthy boundaries that determine how others will be allowed to treat us. Knowledge empowers. Remember, never forget you are precious in God's sight . . . always.

FIGHTING BACK

I put the things I held in my arms away and started to pick up things that were still in one piece. I hung up my shirts, jackets, and pants. The clothes that went in my dresser couldn't be put away because the dresser was also broken into shards that looked like a mad dog had gotten hold of it or my mother had tossed it against the floor four or five times and then kicked it apart from there. Everything that wasn't salvageable I swept into the kitchen by the back door where my mother would have to stumble and trip and (I hoped) fall on her face.

At 11:30 that night in the door she came. And World War III started.

She began screaming, "WHAT THE HELL IS ALL THIS MESS ON THE FLOOR?"

I fired right back: "Just what right do you have doing this to my things? How would you like it if I went into your room and destroyed everything in it?"

The fight was on.

We fought and argued for more than two hours. She lashed out and hit me repeatedly. Finally, I could take no more hitting. I doubled up my fist and fired off one swing at her. I sent her sprawling across the kitchen. I headed out the back door for my car, got in it, and left. Since it was now Monday morning, I headed for the high school.

I pulled into the student parking lot. At least I had my alarm clock with me because I had it at the beach with me over the weekend, so I set it for seven and stretched out in the front seat and went to sleep. For the next three days I did not return home at all. I went to school and then I'd go to work. During this time, I had a chance to sit and think. I figured out I could still cover all the bills at home and still start putting some money away in the bank—just in case I should ever need it.

That Friday, instead of going to school, I went back to the house. I saw that she had taken all the stuff she had destroyed to the garbage and so I unloaded my car, fixed something to eat, then took a long hot shower, set my clock for work, and got some desperately needed sleep. I got in from work at 6 a.m. on Saturday. Guess who was already up drinking coffee? The first thing she said was, "Well, finally decided to come back, huh?"

I told her I was dead tired and I didn't feel like talking about anything, and went in, blocked my door from the inside with a chair and went to bed.

That afternoon, when I got up, she just couldn't wait and immediately began to start her usual routine. She wanted to know where I had been for the last few days, and I just told her, "Around."

She hollered, "Don't get smart with me!"

I wasn't about to tell her where I had spent my free time, because I knew if I had to get away again, she'd know right where to find me. She kept badgering me about where I'd been since the past Friday. I kept giving her the same answer probably ten or so times. I finally verbally lashed, cussed, and started in on her. I very emphatically reminded her who was paying all the bills, who was putting the food on the table, and who was paying for gas for her car so she could go to school. I also loudly let her know that since I was supporting the house, I felt I could pretty well come and go as I damned well pleased and I wasn't beholden to her about my whereabouts in my free time.

Well, I guess you know, that started her up big time and that day went down in flames. She got out the belt and her demon side came into play and I came out the loser. I hurt so badly that I couldn't sleep Saturday night. So I slipped out the back door about 2 a.m., got into my car, and left. I found myself blindly driving around in downtown Fortuna. I don't even remember driving from Rio Dell.

I finally pulled up in my girlfriend's parents' driveway. I eased quietly in, shut off the car so I wouldn't wake anyone up, stretched out in the seat, and went to sleep. I had no idea what time it was. I just thought I needed to go somewhere "safe", and my girlfriend's parent's house fit the bill. What really had me nervous was that I had driven about fifteen miles and had absolutely no memory of it.

By Sunday morning, I now had welts and bruises visible all over me. Mary's mom came out to the car and woke me up. She handed me a cup of coffee and asked me to come in and have something to eat. (Mary's parents were well aware of the type of life I had at home.)

When I tried to get out of my car that morning, I was so stiff and sore I almost dropped the coffee cup and nearly fell on my face. My lower body didn't want to hold up the rest of me and it was not from sleeping in the car. I got inside, pulled up a chair in the kitchen, and began to get myself focused.

Mary's folks asked me if things had gone up in flames again and I said, "Yeah, big time." Mary's dad said, "It looked like it." He was referring to two great big black and blue welts on my right arm, three on my left arm, and a bruise on my right cheek. I excused myself for a minute, went into the bathroom and took my clothes off and started checking myself. From my shoulders to my lower calves, there wasn't much of me that was not bruised or welted. From the looks of it, my mother had really outdone herself this time.

Then Mary knocked on the bathroom door and asked if I was all right. I said I was about as good as could be expected under the circumstances. Mary's mom was there, too. She used to be a nurse and asked if she could see what I looked like. I said okay and they both came in. Mary screamed and almost hit the floor. Her mother turned kind of white, and since Mary had screamed, here came her father to see what was wrong. His face went storm-cloud black and he said the obvious, "S** of a b****! How can a woman do something like this to her own son?"

There was no good answer to that question. Back in those days things like this were not discussed out in the open. It was always kept behind closed doors. As far as I know, back then there weren't laws to cover child abuse, so a person couldn't even call the cops. Kids like me were on their own to make it through childhood as best they could.

GREATER DANGER AND A NEED TO SURVIVE

So much pain. Standing up to his mother never proved a good move for Charles.

This is true for many abuse victims. An abusive parent's ways, typical of most repeat abusers, continue to intensify. The potential for the abused to be in greater danger grows more acute. In turn, there is a deeper need for the abused to become vigilant about personal safety.

All of us instinctively want to feel safe. That blessing should be given from parent to child without question. Since feeling safe at home isn't something abused children can count on, survival measures need to be found. Let's recap things Charles did.

- Charles barricaded the bedroom door
- Charles drove away to his own safe place
- Charles had a supportive group of friends
- Charles made secret plans
- Charles got a job, which meant he had money available

Your list might not look the same as this one. But when survival is at stake, smart moves are necessary. It is also terribly sad to think a boy would need to initiate such extreme measures just to make sure he got to live until the next day.

For Charles, self-preservation had ramped up in a host of practical ways. The older he got, the more danger he sensed, the more he realized some of his paycheck had to be saved for a future time of need. What struck me as remarkable is how he continued to shoulder a sense of responsibility for the household bills. But then, on second thought, to change that up could have ushered in another terrible fight.

By the grace of God this seventeen-year-old, despite the mess he lived in, possessed many good character qualities. There is good in all of us. Tap into the good.

Look outside your home. Not every mother is hateful or raging. There are many kindhearted people, like Mary's parents, who genuinely care and are gentle. Develop good friendships with people who cause you to feel safe enough to relax in their presence.

If you are ready...

Reach for Fresh Joy *[for the abused]*

> Jesus said, "I have loved you even as the
> Father has loved me. Remain in my love."
> John 15:9 NLT

Jesus loves you, not as your mother does, but as God the Father loves Jesus the Son. How would you describe Jesus's love?

_____
_____
_____

Is it hard for you to accept this kind of love? _____

Why? _____
_____
_____

MOTHER'S FURY

The word "remain" is important. What does "remain" imply?
_____
_____
_____

This chapter is a graphic portrayal of a mother who violated her child and his property. Tell of a time when you or your property were violated:
_____
_____
_____

How old were you? _____

What was your reaction?
_____
_____
_____

Jesus was mistreated, too. First Peter 2:21 (NLT) gives us some interesting advice: "For God called you to do good, even if it means suffering, just as Christ suffered for you. He is your example... follow in his steps."

Can you think of a time when Christ suffered? _____
What happened?
_____
_____
_____

Jesus's enemies, many of them religious leaders, wanted to harm Him. And Judas, one of the chosen inner-circle twelve disciples, betrayed him for thirty pieces of silver (Matthew 22:15, 34–35; 26:14–16). Below is a list of possible responses to abuse. Which ones do you believe God would want you to choose? Mark all that apply.

___ Become combative (physically or verbally)

___ Plot revenge

___ Reach out to others

___ Get away from the threat

___ Pray for wisdom

___ Do good to your enemy

Doing *good* might mean not raising your voice, but speaking softly. Walking away from a fight, or choosing to forgive.

The only sure way to wrap one's mind around doing good to an enemy is to start with prayer. Pray to *want* to do good and not to do what you think that person deserves. The natural man or woman will want to strike back. In your own strength, you probably won't desire to be nice to an enemy. But God tells us to pray for our enemies. Bless *yourself* by praying for your abuser. Then set about refocusing that emotional energy to a positive use. Perhaps volunteer time as an advocate for another child who suffers from underserved abuse.

Write out a simple prayer that will enable you to pray for your abuser:

_____
_____
_____
_____
_____
_____

Amen

If you are ready...

Reach for Fresh Hope *[for the abuser]*

> But now you must also rid yourselves
> of all such things as these:
> anger, rage, malice, slander,
> and filthy language from your lips.
> Colossians 3:8

On a scale of 1 to 10 (10 being the worst), how out of control does your anger get? _____

Who have you harmed?

_____
_____
_____

What instructions are found in the Colossians 3:8 verse?
_____

Understand what is being asked of you by writing out a definition for each behavior mentioned.

Anger: _____
_____

Rage: _____
_____

Malice: _____
_____

Slander: _____
_____

Filthy language: _____
_____

Commit Colossians 3:8 to memory. Write it on a sticky note and put it in a place where you will read it several times each day.

> Be bold enough to confess your wrongdoings
> and to ask to be forgiven by those you have hurt.
> Whatever you have learned... put it into practice. And the
> God of peace will be with you. — Philippians 4:9

Being made fun of, teased unmercifully, laughed at, ridiculed, lied about, pushed around, put down, used—all of us have been hurt by another person. And, yes, it *does* hurt. But when you are hurt by someone who is supposed to be there for you—someone like a parent, grandparent, spouse, or caregiver—the pain and the damage are far worse. That kind of hurt causes pain that goes deeper. Pain that feels like it won't ever go away.

Why is the pain so intense? . . . You regarded that person as a vital source of love and comfort and perhaps even protection and care. When a relationship means so much to you, it makes sense that when that relationship goes bad, there is more to lose—and more hurt than normal.[5]

— Dr. Tim Clinton and Dr. Gary Sibcy

FIVE

INVITED TO CHURCH

During this same high school time, my girlfriend Mary invited me to go to church with her. She attended an Assemblies of God church that was known around town as a Holy Roller church. I was really ignorant about churches and at the same time extremely uneasy about even being in a church.

I had been baptized as a Catholic when I was just a year old. When I started kindergarten, I went to Catholic school and, of course, Sunday school, too.

Many were the times Mary and I would have long hard talks about her church. It took a long time for me to understand Mary's interest in religion, but going to church with her meant we could be together. I liked that. My mother did not. She ridiculed me up one side and down the other; I was in the fire all over again. This time, Mary caught hell, too. Mother was convinced Mary was ruining me. She was going to turn me against society. On and on my mother went as if she was up on her own high pulpit preaching at me. Only she wasn't preaching—she was screaming and yelling like a Portuguese fishwife. You could hear her two blocks away!

Despite my mother's disapproval, I did go to church with Mary and I started feeling something happening inside me. I didn't know what, but I was feeling different. I actually took a Bible home from church and began reading it. Then, one day after service, I asked Reverend Murray if he had time to talk with me.

"Come see me Tuesday evening at seven o'clock," he said.

I was there at the appointed time and we talked until almost ten o'clock. Reverend Murray was an easygoing man and equally easy for me to talk to. Over the next few months, we had a dozen talks and then he turned me over to Brother Paul. I had one-on-one sessions with Brother Paul for another three months.

Next I went to meetings geared for people who were just beginning to learn about the Bible. All during this time, it seemed like I could take all of my mother's flak and hatred somewhat easier. It seemed like I had someone there with me taking some of the load. That was strange and yet a source of comfort.

SEEDS OF FAITH

Seeds of faith were sown when his girlfriend invited him to church. He said yes because he wanted to be with her. That's an okay reason to explore a relationship with Jesus. Before long, the church experience was changing him on the inside. He felt a new source of strength, inner calm, and hope. Charles had found himself in a safe, caring place where he could let his guard down. He began to trust that he could share what was on his heart with the church leaders. The Reverend listened and their talks satisfied a hunger deep inside Charles to learn more about God's ways. Their one-on-one meetings continued for many months.

A CRISIS OF FAITH

And then, on the same day I spoke of earlier—the day when my mother destroyed my beloved collections, those 2,000 records left in thousands of broken fragments all over my room, and comic books of Superman, Batman, and the Green Lantern shredded to confetti-sized pieces—I had my first real crisis of faith. I felt so violated.

"Where were you, Lord?" I kept asking. "Why did you let this happen? You abandoned me."

All kinds of crazy, mixed-up things were going through my head. Could my mother have been this upset because I was gone for the weekend? My going off this way was not unusual.

I stood there in the doorway of my room and screamed and yelled like a wolf howling at the ceiling until my throat was sore. Then I went into a really heavy, cold, dark funk. I was so mad I called my mother every terrible name in the book and I cursed God. I kept thinking that if God really cared for his people he wouldn't have let this happen to me.

WHY WOULD GOD ALLOW THIS TO HAPPEN?

The trauma is now more complex because, after believing in God, and trusting in the Lord's protection, his life was still being torn up. Knowing Jesus hadn't stopped his mother from shattering his stuff was hard to accept. If God was so powerful, he wondered, why had he let this terrible wrong happen to him? Could no one protect him or his favorite things? Was he really that unlovable—that worthless? Didn't even God love him? If God loved him, why would a holy God keep allowing his mother to ruin his life?

All valid questions until we come to understand that bad things do happen to good people. Why? Because not everyone practices the Golden Rule. Not everyone treats others as they'd like to be treated themselves. Bad things happened to Jesus. Sometimes bad will happen to us, too. But it's not God's fault. His love endures forever.

Evil exists. Some people are downright mean. Behind that mean spirit is our enemy, the devil, who prowls around looking for ways he can cause believers to reject God, to fall away from their faith. The vile trap gets baited in many ways. By igniting rage in Charles's mother, Satan was able to cause Charles to doubt his faith.

"Gotcha!" he shrieked.

The result was devastating. A dark mood came over Charles. Wasn't it enough to put up with the beatings? He'd grown to expect them. But why were his much-loved collections ruined?

Charles began to blame God as well as his mother.

Evil is not God's fault. People with evil thoughts do bad things—they ravage the innocent. Jesus, in Matthew 12:35, said, "A good man brings good things out of the good stored up in him, and the evil man brings evil things out of the evil stored up in him." God did not make puppets on a string. Rather, God gave people a free will to choose between good and evil, to act in accordance to either his ways or Satan's dirty schemes. The choice is personal. Which one will win out?

If you are ready...

Reach for Fresh Joy *[for the abused]*

> "You are not a God who takes pleasure in evil;
> with you the wicked cannot dwell."
> Psalm 5:4

Have you come to faith in Jesus Christ? _____ Recall when, where, and how that moment came about:

_____
_____
_____
_____

What has your Christian journey been like?

_____
_____
_____
_____

Have you encountered a crisis of faith? _____

If so, write down what caused that crisis to come about?

_____
_____
_____
_____
_____

Philippians 1 finds Paul writing a letter from prison. He is in chains, *not* for doing wrong, but for speaking the truth. Instead of growing bitter, Paul was rejoicing. Read this chapter for yourself. Describe how Paul's words, in verses 27–30, might be acted out in your own life.

_____
_____
_____
_____
_____

If you are ready...

Reach for Fresh Hope *[for the abuser]*

> "Then the LORD said to Cain,
> 'Why are you angry? Why is your face downcast?
> If you do what is right, will you not be accepted?
> But if you do not do what is right,
> sin is crouching at your door; it desires to have you,
> but you must rule over it.'"
> Genesis 4:6–7

A misuse of anger is a very old problem. Its misuse has plagued people down through the centuries. And now you are the one needing to master the conspirator's deplorable schemes.

Let's dig into the above verse. What is God's first question?
_____

How would you answer that question?
_____

What will it take for you to be accepted?
_____

What would "doing right" require of you?
_____

Those interested in pursuing a particular career path know certain skills must be mastered in order to achieve their goal. Mastering anger takes training and tenacity, too. Anything worth having requires an all-out effort. Otherwise, that high-paying job will not be yours. God warns that _____ is crouching at your door. Will you continue to open your door to sin?_____

Write a short prayer asking the Lord to help you master your anger:
_____
_____
_____
_____

Perhaps you have heard people talking about the "love of God" through the years, and somehow it just didn't have any meaning for you. You heard people say, "God loves you" or "Jesus loves you" or "God has a wonderful plan for your life," but it was just so many words.

But then there came a moment when you suddenly realized that message was just for you. Suddenly the light came on, and you realized that the whole choir was singing for you, that heaven was waiting for you, that Jesus Christ died on a Roman cross for you. And in that moment your eyes opened wide, your mouth dropped open, and you said, "This is for me. This means me!"[6]

— Ron Mehl

Six

Finding My Father

A lot happened when I was seventeen and still going with Mary. I had been able to finally get in touch with my father. That came about with the unexpected help of Mr. Maxwell, a men's clothing store-owner in Rio Del. He had me do odd jobs for him every now and then. One day, he just happened to ask me about the fact that he noticed there seemed to be no man around the house. I told him my parents divorced when I was only five.

He began to ask me if I knew anything about my father.

I said, "No."

He asked, "Do you know where he lives?"

Again I said, "No."

Mr. Maxwell asked, "Has your father ever been in the military?"

To that I said, "Yes."

"What branch?"

"The army," I replied.

Mr. Maxwell had some friends in the Pentagon.

"Would you like to talk to your father?" he asked.

My answer was the world's fastest, "Yes!"

"Would you mind if I made some inquiries about your father?"

"Sure!" I said. "Give it your best shot."

Two days later, Mr. Maxwell called me to come by his store. He had located my father. I went to his office. Sticking out from under his desk phone was a piece of paper with my father's name, address, and both home and work phone numbers on it. He'd taken the matter further and had just talked to my father who'd been living in Columbus, Georgia, since 1955. I learned that my dad was at work right now and I was to call that number.

Mr. Maxwell said, "Your dad is eagerly waiting to hear from you."

I was so excited! That phone was picked up lightning fast and I dialed the number. Of course, my father, being at work, had to answer the phone in a formal manner. But as soon as I said, "Dad, it's me, Charlie," there was an immediate shared and precious silence that hung between us.

Then I heard my dad start to cry. It took him a few moments to regain his composure. When the words came, we were on the phone for about an hour. This went down in memory as one of the best days of my entire life—a day I had thought would never come.

A WELCOMED BLESSING

Some of you may also long to hear from an absentee parent. Don't give up hope.

A father and son reunited is a beautiful thing. What a long overdue blessing tucked into this story. It wasn't God's idea for this relationship to be torn apart. And so great was the fear of coming in contact with his explosive ex-wife that he'd kept his distance. He knew what she was capable of doing.

Her vile temper had kept father and son apart for twelve long years. Now that contact was reestablished, neither of them wanted to risk being caught in the crosshairs of her angry moods and dangerous outbursts. That never ended well.

Mother could never know.

Questions roll through our minds. It will remain a mystery why this dad, who loved his son and bravely served his country, didn't fight for custody years earlier.

Fortunately, there are caring individuals like Mr. Maxwell, who chose to act on behalf of this teen. His good deed was spot-on. Let's not forget Mr. Maxwell. He encourages the rest of us to either believe lost relationships can be found or to go that extra mile. Someday, a situation where our sphere of influence can lend a hand, add hope, and change a life just might pop up.

THE HELP OF A CARING FRIEND

I couldn't help but think what would happen if my mother ever found out about this. She would kill me.

Mother could never know. Not ever!

Amy (Dad's lady friend and square dance partner), Dad, and I made a way for me to call him as much as I wanted without my mother finding out. Again, Mr. Maxwell was part of the plan. He let me use his phone whenever I wanted to without ever paying for a call. Letters flew back and forth, too. The address I used was Maxwell's Clothing Store. Mr. Maxwell made a place on his desk under the phone for me to pick up my "mail."

This continued without my mother ever knowing about it.

One thing my mother had always done, all through the years, was to put my father down. He was always a no-good this, a no-good that, and every other kind of degrading remark that had all kinds of toxic filthy language in them.

When my mother was in one of her routine moods from hell and was beating me into the floor, she would always compare me with my dad and always say we were both alike—that we were no good—and call the two of us every kind of maligning insulting name she could come up with. With her being ex-military, she had a vocabulary that could melt steel.

THE PAIN OF PARENT ALIENATION

Parent Alienation Syndrome (the name given to one parent pitting a child against the other) is a cruel act of selfishness that is not in the best interests of the child. For one parent to act out with extreme loathing against the other biological parent (their ex) is blatant verbal abuse. To use words of hateful comparison of a child to an estranged father or mother does great damage to the youngster's self-image. The child comes to believe that because he is related to the perceived "bad" parent, that he, too, is no good. This is a terribly unfair burden for a boy or girl to carry.

The obvious payback for any parent participating in such alienation is that of selfish, vengeful satisfaction. No regard is given to the child's well-being. Verbal abuse sticks on the tender heart of the child like peanut butter does when it is smeared on bread. Once stuck to the surface, it would be really hard to scrape off. While the peanut butter sandwich provides good nourishment, parent alienation does the complete opposite. It feeds the spirit of heaviness and poor self-esteem.

A CLOSE BOND GREW

From 1967 to 1980, my dad and I really built a close father-son bond through phone calls and letters. Taking into consideration he was in Columbus (Fort Benning), Georgia, and I was in Eureka, California, and later in Medford, Oregon, it was the best we could do.

I learned my dad had come from a family of seven sons and one daughter and that I had no siblings.

During WWII, while stationed in Korea, my father had his legs knocked out from under him by shrapnel from a mortar round that exploded close to him. He was medevac'd out by medics and treated for immediate needs and then sent back to the States for further surgeries and other treatments. The shrapnel had damaged some of the veins and capillaries in his legs and so parts of his veins and capillaries had to be replaced with tubing. He eventually recovered from his injuries and resumed his military career.

All was moving ahead nicely with our relationship.

If you are ready...

Reach for Fresh Joy *[for the abused]*

"In that wonderful day you will sing:
'Thank the Lord! Praise his name!
Tell the nations what he has done.
Let them know how mighty he is!"
Isaiah 12:4 NLT

Below: Choose the path to fresh joy that fits your current circumstances. One is for those who have reunited with a parent and the other is for those who still hope to reunite with a parent.

Did you reunite with an absentee parent? _____

When? _____

How did that relationship restart?
_____
_____
_____
_____
_____
_____

"I will sing to the Lord because he is good to me."
Psalm 13:6 NLT

Write a prayer of praise to the Lord:
_____
_____
_____
_____
_____
_____

Do you long to reunite with an absentee parent? _____

What steps have you already taken?
_____
_____
_____
_____
_____

What are your expectations?
_____
_____
_____
_____
_____

Will you give the Lord veto power over your desire to reunite with that parent? _____

"A man's heart plans his way, but the Lord directs his steps."
Proverbs 16:9 NKJV

Seek God's will. Write a prayer that both speaks the desire of your heart and wisely leaves the outcome up to God. Sometimes God doesn't open a door because more pain could follow.

_____
_____
_____
_____
_____
_____
_____
_____
_____
_____
_____

If you are ready...

Reach for Fresh Hope *[for the abuser]*

> "Anyone who is among the living has hope—
> even a live dog is better off than a dead lion!"
> Ecclesiastes 9:4

Yes, you've messed up when it comes to parenting. But you are alive and therefore have hope.

Time is on your side. But don't put off making changes that can heal family relationships.

Children do best when they have access to both parents. Why didn't you want your child to have a relationship with the other parent?

_____
_____
_____
_____

What did you do to prevent him/her contact with that parent?

_____
_____
_____
_____

Dig deeper. Examine any unresolved bitter feelings toward your ex. What do you discover?

_____
_____
_____

Unless there is a clear danger, parent alienation harms children. Will you choose to stop putting down your ex, to stop the name-calling and hate-infused talk? _____

What will you do to show your son or daughter it's okay to love the other parent?

_____
_____
_____

Pray. Ask for God's help. He wants you to succeed. With His help, you can.

> "Those who hope in the Lord will renew their strength.
> They will soar on wings like eagles;
> they will run and not grow weary,
> they will walk and not be faint."
> Isaiah 40:31

No has two faces [the word "no"]: The one we turn toward ourselves and the one that creates boundaries between ourselves and others. When it protects you from abuse by others. Sadly, our most important relationships often invite our ugliest communications. In part that's because the people closest to us arouse our strongest emotions, and in part it's because they are the people we fear losing the most. Fear can sap the strength we need to say *No*, just when we need that power the most.[7]

— Judith Sills, Ph.D.

SEVEN

MOTHER'S NEW HOBBY

In 1967, the year I turned eighteen and was about to graduate from high school, my mother took up a new hobby. Her hobby was fish tanks full of fish. She started with the obvious one tank and had three within a month. She took care of those tanks most of the time, but once in a while I got the job of cleaning the tanks. To this day, I suspect her real interest in aquariums was to find another reason to keep me at home.

Then one day a guy she knew from the college came over to build her a custom shelf for the tanks. Our house in Rio Dell was huge inside. The front room was forty-eight feet on each wall. The kitchen was thirty-five feet on each wall. The bathroom you could get lost in. Both bedrooms were twenty-eight feet on each side.

The fish tank shelf was installed along one of the long kitchen walls because the kitchen sink was nearby to make cleaning the tanks a lot easier. My mother started to think that since the shelf was so long, and had three tiers, that maybe she'd get a couple more tanks. Only those tanks were just a little larger. Then about four months later someone she knew gave her their old sixty-gallon tank.

By now you are asking what the fish story has to do with the rest of this. Well read on to hear, as Paul Harvey used to say, "The Rest of the Story."

While she collected fish tanks, I took an interest in bottle collecting. I found all kinds of bottles of different shapes, colors, design work, and most of all custom whiskey decanters. I filled them with sterilized colored water and put them on windowsills. With the sunlight shining through them, they were really pretty.

By early 1969, I had about seventy-five bottles all over the house. I also had them (unfortunately) in the kitchen on the windowsill over the sink. By now my mother's fish tanks had grown from only five to thirty-five. She had a 100-gallon tank, three fifty-gallon tanks, four twenty-fives and eight twenty-gallon tanks. All the rest were five and ten-gallon tanks spread out on this custom-made three-tiered shelf. More and more often I was getting stuck taking care of the tanks because my mother was too involved in her schooling or going to all-night parties with people she knew.

I didn't think it was right or proper for her to slide all the work down on me just because she always had to go party or invoke some other idiotic excuse. Yeah, kids can get just as sick and tired of excuses from parents as parents get sick and tired of hearing them from kids.

HEY! I DESERVE SOME PRIVACY

Midway through 1969 I was still working, saving money, and still getting regular beatings for not cleaning her fish tanks. They became a real stressful point of conflict between us. Add to it that by now my mother had gotten real crafty, underhanded, and sneaky when it came to finding out where I went when I'd take *off. She found out where I hung out at the beach and where some of my friends lived.*

She found out about some of the places I hung out in Eureka, and worst of all, she found out where Mary lived. She threw that in my face one night during one of our usual rows. I was blown out of the water to say the least. But I tried to keep a straight face so she wouldn't know I was caught off guard with that one. She was half-liquored up that night and really feeling proud of herself that she had pulled the rug out from under me.

So she kept right on running her drunken mouth and told me she'd had people watching me for months. She was brazen enough to tell me who the people were, how they followed me, and all the juicy little details of her spy network.

The old adage, "Being forewarned is being forearmed," worked real well for me because I quit taking the same streets as I always had. I began to watch my rearview mirror and, if I thought I was being followed, I learned how to lose those tails within a mile or two just so I could have a real good laugh at the expense of all those idiots and my mother.

I'd get my gas tank filled and deliberately lead those people all over Fortuna and Eureka and even to Arcata. I was having some real fun letting those morons follow me and then they'd go back and tell my mother they had nothing to report. I thought that was hilarious because I was making a monkey out of them all.

But when I did have a specific place to go, I made double-sure that I got where I was going without a shadow on me. The fox was outfoxing the hound! But even that had serious repercussions on me every once in a while. And it would start with the obvious.

She'd ask, "Where the hell were you last night?"

My usual reply was, "Out with friends." Or I'd just say, "Out." Those answers seemed to really set her off like dynamite. Then I'd remind her that since I was the head of the house—and the only one keeping all the bills paid—I had the right to come and go as I pleased. She never agreed with that one.

But truth is I was working and paying all the bills. I deserved a little privacy in my life. To come and go as I pleased was all I asked for or wanted. But did I get that? No way!

I was standing up for myself and defying my mother more and more. She refused to see me as a grown-up. Some lessons and battles were hard fought. Some were won and some were lost. I was working like an adult, earning the money of a man, and I was going to be treated as one. That's all there was to it.

My mother was now doing a lot of partying and even drinking a lot at home. Usually it was beer and wine; once in a while, hard booze. She couldn't hold her brew very well and was more of an out-of-control monster boozed up than when she was sober. When she would light into me, I would come out hurting a lot worse when she was bombed than when she was sober. A couple times I landed in the hospital with injuries from some of her insane tirades and beatings.

THE FINAL BATTLE

Two months after my twentieth birthday, the worst and final battle took place and it was all because of those fish tanks. It was the tail end of the second week of June 1969 at 6:30 a.m. We were both up and she was just about ready to head out the door to school. I was getting ready to make something to eat and then *watch TV for a while. Well, mother dear really screwed up my plans. Hey, it was Friday! No school. The mill was down for some repairs and wouldn't be running until the next week. So I had some unexpected extra time to burn.*

Being Friday, it was also payday. As soon as she left, I went and picked up my check, and came back home. What my mother had demanded—she didn't ask—was that I clean all the fish tanks and have all of them cleaned by the time she got home or there would be hell to pay. Why me? Why did I have to clean all of them today? Remember, there were thirty-five tanks. Some were huge. Well I got nine small tanks cleaned before the banks opened, and I stopped only long enough to run two blocks down the street and cash my check. This check was totally free and clear and I thought tonight I would take my girlfriend out to dinner, a movie, and maybe go park on the beach for a couple of hours.

I got back from the bank and back to cleaning the fish tanks. I was doing a total strip, clean, and sterilize of all the tanks so it took lots of hot water. I did the 100-gallon tank first, then the fifty-gallon tanks. By the time I got them done, I was out of hot water and had to wait for the water heater to recover. By about 4:15, I had only four ten-gallon tanks left to clean, but I was out of hot water again. So I cleaned up the kitchen drain boards and hung up the towels I had been using. I hung a large bath towel I had been setting the tanks on as I dried them over a chair.

Twenty minutes later there was enough hot water for a really quick shower. With that done, I put on some of my good clothes, a nice western shirt, Levis and my boots. I called Mary and asked her if she was busy and if she would like to go out tonight. OK. The plans were all made.

Mother dear came in just a little after five and first thing she said was, "Where are you all dressed up to go?" I told her. Next, she wanted to know if the tanks were done. I told her I only had four tanks to go and that I was out of hot water. I also added that I would finish them the next day. That didn't seem like an unusual thing to me.

She slammed her books down on the table and started screaming at me. She demanded that I get them done now and that I wasn't going anywhere until the tanks were done. I again repeated that the next day was Saturday and I'd finish them then.

She screamed, "YOU'LL DO THEM NOW, MISTER!"

I had worked on those things for eleven and a half hours. For one day, that was more than enough and I told her so.

She growled, "YOU LITTLE MOTHER F****R, I'll teach you to argue with me." With that she headed for her room and came back with the belt. She swung it at me.

Without even thinking, I grabbed it, jerked it out of her hand, went to the silverware drawer, pulled out a butcher knife, and within a heartbeat I had cut that belt into four tiny little pieces about a foot long and threw them at her.

"Let's see you do something with the belt now, you maniac," I said.

She actually turned purple. She let out a scream, looked around the kitchen, reached up on the windowsill and grabbed one of my decorative decanter bottles. The bottles I had collected.

She took the bottle by the neck and before I could react, she spun on her heel and swung the bottle at me. She hit me right square in the middle of my lower lip and blood immediately flew all over the place. She laid my lower lip open with the bottom of the bottle. I let out a howl of pain you could have heard near a block away and called her about fifteen very insulting names.

I was now totally on remote control (or autopilot or something). I grabbed the bath towel off the back of the kitchen chair, blood pouring down the front of my forty dollar western shirt, and went out the door to my car. My car was a typical hot rod; a '57 Ford station wagon with a transplanted 400-horse engine, nose-down, tail-up hot rod, capable of an easy 140 miles an hour on the freeway.

All the while, Mother was screaming, "GET BACK HERE OR I'LL CALL THE POLICE ON YOU."

I hollered, "GO AHEAD, I DON'T CARE. THEY'LL NEVER CATCH ME IN THIS CAR."

I got in, fired it up and smoked it out the driveway into the street and down the block, and was gone. All the while the towel I was holding to my mouth was getting more and more soaked in blood, ruining the originally snowball white fabric; it was beginning to look like it was tie-dyed in blood. I maintained about a 105 miles an hour all the way out the freeway back to Fortuna.

Where were the cops? Not a one in sight, anywhere.

SHOWING UP AT MARY'S HOUSE

Shock began settling in on me from the loss of blood. I took a shortcut through the south end of Fortuna to Mary's house, the only place I could clearly think of going. I came sliding into her driveway at about fifty miles per hour and the dust flew. I almost hit Mary's dad's car. I made enough commotion sliding into the driveway that everyone came flying out the door. Her dad was the first one to the car.

All I could say was, "HIDE THE CAR! HIDE MY CAR! I DON'T WANT MY MOTHER TO FIND IT."

Mary, her mother, and her two sisters helped me into the house. I was almost off my feet from shock. Mary's father immediately took my car down behind their house where he cut the firewood and parked it in among the giant ferns and redwood trees. My car was dark green. It blended in.

They got me into the bathroom, took off my shirt and started cleaning me up. Afterward Mary's dad helped take me to the back of the house and put me in bed. Her mother kept doing something to my mouth. I wasn't in much shape to know much of anything. I woke up later, later than I thought, and found Mary sitting on the foot of the bed on one side and her mother on the other side.

The first thing her mother asked was, "How do you feel?"

I said my head was exploding and my mouth hurt. At least that's what I tried to say. Everything came out a little slurred because my lower lip was about three times its normal size and it hurt like hell. As I slowly became aware of my surroundings, I was brought up to speed on everything that had happened since I came sliding in the driveway the day before. I was shocked to realize it was now Saturday and a little after two in the afternoon.

Mary told me her dad had hidden my car down behind the house in the firewood pit. I tried to snicker about that because I immediately realized that down there no one would find my car unless they were right down in that hollow.

Her mother started laughing about seeing the "old man" behind the wheel of my car. She also told me how they actually went out and seriously searched the entire driveway and scuffed out every tire track from my car they could find. Then I was told about how they cleaned me up and got the bleeding stopped and how Mary's mother had stitched my lip back together to stop the bleeding with suture needles from their first aid kit.

I found out my mother had come by six times and drove back and forth, then would leave, then come back by later. Mary said they had really expected my mother to stop and come to the door, but she never did. Mary's mom showed me my shirt. She was able to get the blood out because it was still wet and even the towel was almost spotless. Mary's dad came in with a glass in his hand.

"Belt it down," he said. "It will help clear your head and get you up on your feet in about a half an hour."

He was right. I recognized the Jack Daniels in the glass and, yes, it started clearing my head almost as soon as it hit bottom. Within a short while, with a little help, I was out at the kitchen table with all the curtains facing the driveway closed so if mother dear came by, I wouldn't be seen. I sat there and enjoyed the most delicious cup of coffee in the world. That was the first cup I'd had since the morning before when I had my breakfast just after mother left for school.

That evening, Mary's folks went downtown and ordered out for our dinner. They brought back three king-sized pizzas, and we had our own little night out for dinner on the back porch in the sunset—all seven of us. I spent the rest of the weekend at their house. They wouldn't allow me to leave as long as there was a possibility that I might bump into the battle-ax, as they called her. So I spent a very wonderful weekend with Mary and her family.

ALL-CONSUMING RAGE

So much rage! Physical battering had ramped up to a more dangerous level. Reading this story, it's a wonder Charles Rice lived to see his nineteenth birthday. This kind of all-consuming rage and vile loathing can trigger the most horrific of outcomes—even murder. Again, the onslaught of foul language and violence from the mother quickly fueled a parallel blind rage in the son. Vicious deplorable words, hitting, and crazy wild actions turned into a brutal, bloody brawl.

It's not possible to reason with a furious mother. She wants to win—at all costs. Long after puberty, after all signs of the boy gave way to manhood, the rage toward him continued no different than what's seen in the rhythmic pattern of the ocean's waves.

CREATE A SAFE PLACE

Charles was smart enough to choose escape—to get out of the house when he did. His car was ready and he was gone! With adrenaline coursing through his veins at such an elevated level, this presented another danger. His driving that day could have led to a very bad car crash. Innocent people could have been hurt. Fortunately, that didn't happen. It's probable that God's angels were watching over him. However it happened, he got his wits about him and found his way to his safe place.

Anyone who is the target of an abuser needs a safe haven to hunker down when abuse spirals to life-threatening levels.

Think of this basic necessity no differently than planning for a fire drill. Smart families plan ahead. In case of a house fire, they all know to get out of the house and to meet in a preplanned place to escape the danger. This might mean meeting under the oak tree near the corner of the property. Why? Because it's the safest place to be.

For the abused, the relationship is a constant, smoldering bed of hot coals. At any moment an inferno has the potential to ignite—and with little to no warning. Having a prearranged covert plan of escape ready to act upon can mean the difference between life and death.

Staying safe, staying alive, starts with a caring and trusted third party—someone who is smart enough to keep your hiding place a secret. If possible, have access to a getaway car and money enough to get by on for an indefinite period of time. Above all, believe that staying alive may well depend on who you choose as a personal advocate and how masterful you are at crafting a plan of escape.

If you are ready...

Reach for Fresh Joy *[for the abused]*

"Be on your guard; stand firm in the faith;
be courageous; be strong."
1 Corinthians 16:13

God wants you to be alert to what is happening around you. What measures have you taken to ensure your own safety?

_____
_____
_____

Who has helped/is helping you along the way (advocate or confidant)?

_____
_____
_____

If you need a personal advocate, who might you ask to assume that role?

_____
_____
_____

Did you choose anger as a coping mechanism in your early years? _____

How well did that work for you? _____
What was the result?

_____
_____
_____

Anger often becomes a reactive, go-to powerful and addictive behavior. Ephesians 4:26 says: "'In your anger do not sin': Do not let the sun go down while you are still angry."

Is it okay to be angry? _____

The Bible tells us to do what with our anger?
_____
_____

What changes need to take place for you to put this verse into practice?
_____
_____

> "The tongue also is a fire, a world of evil among the parts of the body. It corrupts the whole body, sets the whole course of one's life on fire, and is itself set on fire by hell."
> James 3:6

Words have the power to build up or tear down, to add blessings or inflict pain. Why is it important to understand the significance of angry words?
_____
_____
_____

When we remember God's wisdom, especially in moments of anger, and act upon His teachings, life's wrongs are lots easier to bear.

Write a short prayer asking the Lord to help you *not* to sin when you feel angry:

___
___
___
___

If you are ready...

Reach for Fresh Hope *[for the abuser]*

"The tongue also is a fire, a world of evil among the parts of the body. It corrupts the whole body, sets the whole course of one's life on fire, and is itself set on fire by hell."
James 3:6

Oh how words spoken in anger hurt others. What were you hoping to accomplish with such disrespectful talk?

___
___
___

Do you often put unrealistic expectations on your children?
___

List some of those expectations:
___

Do you allow your child an opportunity to speak his/her thoughts? _____

Why or why not?
_____
_____

Have you been physically abusive to your son or daughter?
_____

What triggers that abuse?
_____
_____

What wounds did you inflict?
_____
_____

How did you feel later?
_____
_____

Words have the power to build up or tear down, to add blessings or inflict pain. Words followed by beatings are even more damaging. Why is it important to understand the significance of angry wods?
_____
_____
_____
_____

> "Let the wicked forsake their ways and the
> unrighteous their thoughts.
> Let them turn to the Lord, and
> he will have mercy on them, and
> to our God, for he will freely pardon."
>
> Isaiah 55:7

You have a temper! There is nothing unique about that. Most people have tempers, in varying degrees, of course. God does not ask that you get rid of that temper. But He does say that if you are to be happy, it must be brought under control and rechanneled to proper use. God cannot use a man without a temper as well as one with a controlled temper. Too many professed Christians never get "wrought up" about anything; they never get indignant with injustice, with corruption in high places, or with the godless traffics which barter away the souls and bodies of men. Daily prayer: Use my anger to help others, Lord. When I see them hurting or Your world decaying, let me be challenged to reach out—instead of merely exploding.

> Jonah 4:4 But the Lord replied,
> "Is it right for you to be angry?"

— *Day by Day with Billy Graham*, Sept 28th
("Tame Your Temper")

EIGHT

"I'm Outta Here!"

At dinnertime, that same Sunday, Mary's mom asked me some loaded questions I wasn't expecting and didn't know how to answer.

"How much longer are you going to put up with the abuse?" she asked. "When are you going to do something about it? What are your plans now—since all this has happened?"

All of a sudden I had some really heavy-duty thinking to do.

ASK TOUGH QUESTIONS

Some of us will find it surprising that Charles hadn't seriously considered this idea on his own. But when one steps back to look at his childhood history, we realize abuse was what he'd grown up with; that being beat up was his normal. He knew nothing else. How could he? Charles had been battered from the day Daddy left. His mother beat him up. He had miraculously survived. The wounds would scar over and the tumultuous cycle would repeat. As crazy as that sounds, this was the only life he knew. Breaking away from his abuser hadn't crossed his mind until now.

When did he begin to think differently? Only after a concerned friend, in this case Mary's mom, stepped up and asked the tough questions that needed answering. He began to consider change.

It is not unusual for abuse victims to believe they are unable to break free of an abuser. And if they can imagine such a change, it's likely they'll need help to figure out how.

FORGE A PLAN OF ESCAPE

About nine o'clock that night I began discussing the problem with them. I really couldn't come up with any ideas on my own. I made it known that I really didn't feel comfortable, or safe, going back home anymore. I knew I would have to get out now, but where to? I knew if I stayed in the area my mother would undoubtedly continue to torment my life or threaten my safety.

We all tossed around the idea of relocating somewhere else where the battle-ax wouldn't be able to find me. That sounded workable, but then Mary started getting panicky. Right in front of her parents, she hit me with the 64,000-dollar question. "If you leave . . . then what about you and me?"

Now there were more new questions to be answered, more pieces to the puzzle. My first reaction was, "If I go somewhere else, I guess I'll have to go alone." Boy was that a wrong answer. Mary said if I went anywhere she wanted to go with me. In less than a minute, we had both put our foot in our mouths right in front of her folks. They immediately picked up on the intensity in Mary's voice and looked at each other and then they both looked at us.

Her mom smiled a little sheepishly but her dad's look was more like, "have you two been doing something that maybe we should know about?" The silence in the room almost muffled out the TV. Mary and I had been having sexual relations for almost a year. She was just ready to turn eighteen and I was now nineteen.

Mary's mom broke the silence. She asked Mary if she really wanted to go with me if I decided to leave the area.

Mary immediately and very emphatically said, "Yes."

Once again there was the look from her mom and dad. This time it passed almost as fast as it had appeared.

Mary's dad then asked, "If Mary goes with you, will you protect her and take care of her?"

I answered, "Yes!"

At that point, a plan started to fall into place. The first step was to figure out how I should go about getting my stuff out of the house. We devised a plot based on the idea that my mother would go to school as usual on Monday.

On Monday, Mary and I were up before the birds and chickens. By 6:30 we were about a block away and behind the house where we could see without being seen. And sure as shootin' right at 7 a.m., my mother left the house. We waited for half an hour in case she showed back up. When we felt we were in the clear, we pulled in and I backed the car up to the back door and we went in and started pulling out what few things I still had. We hurriedly threw everything in and were all loaded up and out of my driveway in less than an hour. When we left, my room was totally bare. We headed back to Mary's house where her mom and dad helped pull everything out of my car and repack it in an organized fashion.

Mary's five suitcases and other things were packed and the car was ready to go.

The parting was tearful because Mary was coming with me. The two of us were leaving the area without a real idea of where we'd go. I filled the car with gas and headed north. There was some kind of halfway fitting feeling as we headed toward Eureka because we had to go right past College of the Redwoods. It felt to me like, "Hey Mom. Kiss my behind! I'm outta here!"

The drive that day was slow and leisurely. There was a little sightseeing along the way in Klamath, California, and also at the Trees of Mystery. Finally, we stopped for the night in Crescent City.

I had phoned in my resignation to Pacific Lumber Company and had my last check in cash in my pocket. By Monday, the two of us were getting settled in Grants Pass, Oregon. My savings account was soon transferred to a local bank.

The move north was clearly a good decision. Mary and I had begun our life together. By the start of the next week, I'd landed a real good paying job in a lumber mill just a few blocks from where we were living. Things went really good for us for about the first year. Then the absolutely unexpected happened.

One midsummer afternoon, while shopping at the downtown Safeway store, just as we rounded the corner of an aisle, I let go of the cart, grabbed Mary, and jerked her back to where we had just been. Mary got upset with me and wanted to know what was wrong. I told her to take a careful peek around the corner and then tell me what she saw. She didn't have to say a word. I heard her sharp intake of breath and her low and quiet, "Oh my gosh!" Yep! You guessed it. There she stood: my battle-ax mother, looking at canned veggies.

Mary and I instantly panicked. We left our cart full of groceries behind, made a quick beeline for the front door, got in the car, and left like a flash of lightning. A couple of blocks away our breathing returned to normal. We both shared the same unspoken thought. "What is she doing up here?"

After doing our grocery shopping at another store, we returned home to call Mary's folks and tell them what had happened. They were shocked far worse than the two of us—if that was even possible. What was really strange was that she knew my car with just a glance. How in the world did she miss it when it was parked right in front of the main doors? My car was a one of a kind in Eureka and Fortuna because of the way it was painted and fixed up, and it was also a one of a kind in Grants Pass. That car was a class act just sitting in a parking lot.

Things quieted down and that incident didn't reoccur for almost a year. Then it happened again! This time my mother saw us! Her face went lividly scarlet and stormy. Right then and there she started making a very unsightly, highly embarrassing, spectacle right there in the grocery store.

We hadn't even said anything to her. So back out the door we went and to the car and back home. This time we waited until the next day to do our shopping. Both of us were really getting freaked out because of the two unwelcomed encounters. Were we being stalked?

We pulled up stakes. I turned in my resignation at work. We packed up and moved on—this time thirty miles away to Medford.

Things went well for about five years before the unthinkable slipped in again. In three days' time, we bumped into my mother four times. Once at a theater, a grocery store, Bi-Mart, and a

Laundromat. This was too freaky to overlook or shrug off. Our lurking suspicions began to take form and become a reality. We no longer imagined we were being followed; we knew we were being followed. The worst part of the whole equation was how did she know we moved to Oregon? How did she know we lived in Grants Pass? How did she end up in Medford?

PURSUED AND TORMENTED

Escaping an abuser is not always as simple as driving away from the scene of the abuse to get a fresh start hundreds of miles up the road. If that person is unrelenting—as was the case with Charles's mother, the hunter pursuing the hunted—she continues to torment her prey. There's no intent to back down. The controlling maneuvers only shift from in-home verbal and physical beatings to stalking and creating mental anguish.

RELATIONSHIPS SUFFER

The flashbacks were unstoppable. It kept coming back to me how my mother had once gloated about how she had people watching me. I told Mary about that. She turned physically cold to the touch.

Mary and I spent eight years together. During our last four years, my mother sought us out. At first, she behaved in a halfway friendly manner and a tiny shoot of hope for change began to grow. Of course, everything has to come to an end. After two years of some type of friendship, Mother went back to her old self. The same old problems started up all over again. Mary finally broke under the emotional load and returned to Fortuna, California, and to her parents.

In 1976, I married Sharon. Ten years later we were divorced and she passed away in 1987. After three more years, Linda and I married. One day she asked about my parents. I told her the whole ball of wax. She thought it was pretty ridiculous. I agreed. Linda wasn't one to put up with my mother's tricks and would tell her off. Again, this marriage was doomed; after eight years another divorce.

EMOTIONALLY WOUNDED

Charles Rice had not grown up witnessing a healthy marriage relationship between a mother and father that he could one day emulate, respect, or remotely admire. His experience is the norm for those living with abuse. What they are generally exposed to is poor parenting, horrid maltreatment, and a string of strangers parading in and out of the bedroom door.

When we add up those childhood negatives, there's a clear picture of a guy who was well prepared to enter adulthood an emotionally wounded man. In stature he grew up, as we all do, but the significance of his psychological wounds—and the power they held to negatively influence the outcome of future relationships—had not yet been figured out.

Children from abusive homes are more prone to broken relationships during their lifetime. The basics of loving parental nurturing are so important to our well-being later in life. When that component is missing, the child suffers great loss and is at greater risk of repeating the abuse cycle. It will be hard to both receive love and give love.

The Oklahoma Coalition Against Domestic Violence and Sexual Assault *www.ocadvsa.org/dv_children.htm* reports that:
Boys from homes where domestic violence is present:

- Are four times more likely to abuse in a dating relationship.

- Are twenty-five times more likely to commit rape as an adult.

- Are six times more likely to commit suicide.

- Have a 74% greater chance of committing crimes against others.

- And are 1,000 times more likely to commit violent acts against their own children.

Statistics like this make it incredibly important for abuse victims to hunger after help. There is no question that the damage done in childhood was unfair. It was not your fault. You were an innocent child born into unfortunate parenting. But if you don't seek help, those statistics may become a reality.

Face the truth. When a parent doesn't give love or display anger appropriately, the child grows up with a host of damaged emotions. Those feelings of being worthless and undervalued need to be healed. Proper conflict resolution skills have got to be learned. These steps will take time. Begin by grabbing hold of God's truth. Trust that He will help you acquire suitable life skills; many are found in His word. Believe that a positive future can rise from the ashes of a damaged childhood.

If you are ready...

Reach for Fresh Joy *[for the abused]*

"Do not gloat over me, my enemy!
Though I have fallen, I will rise.
Though I sit in darkness, the LORD will be my light"
Micah 7:8

Fear works two ways. It can be anticipated or it can come upon us in an instant and become a paralyzing experience. Has fear ever surprised you? _____ Describe what happened:
_____
_____
_____

How did you react?
_____
_____
_____

In Acts 22:18 (NKJV) God told Paul to "take haste and get out of Jerusalem quickly, for they will not receive your testimony concerning Me." Murder was on the minds of Paul's enemies (verse 22).

Does this passage give you courage? _____
_____
_____

How might God be speaking to you about escaping your enemy/abuser?

_____
_____
_____
_____
_____

Or, if you did escape, take a moment to express thanks to God for planting that idea in your mind and making a way out for you:

_____
_____
_____
_____
_____

Has a close "love" relationship suffered because of your damaged emotions? _____
_____

How?

_____
_____
_____
_____
_____

If you are ready...

Reach for Fresh Hope *[for the abuser]*

"My people have committed two sins;
They have forsaken me, the spring of living water,
and have dug their own cisterns,
broken cisterns that cannot hold water."
Jeremiah 2:13

Would you agree that you've been living life your way with no regard to God's will?
_____
_____

How has that worked out for you?
_____
_____

Describe the relationship you have with your child:
_____
_____
_____

Look again at the Oklahoma statistics near the end of this chapter. What do those mean to you?
_____
_____
_____

Were you previously aware of contributing to your child being at greater risk of suicide, committing criminal acts, or one day growing up to be an abuser, too? _____

How does that make you feel?
_____
_____

Have you continued to inflict emotional abuse or stalked your child even after he's chosen to leave home? _____

What are some of the things you have done?
_____
_____

Do you feel genuine sorrow for your actions? _____

Will you choose to repent? _____

If so, write a prayer seeking forgiveness and self-discipline to do what's right by your child:
_____
_____

> "This is what the LORD says: 'If you repent,
> I will restore you that you may serve me;
> if you utter worthy, not worthless, words,
> you will be my spokesman.'"
> Jeremiah 15:19

Hold your abusers accountable but do not blame them. The purpose of acknowledging what really happened to you is to end the unconscious conspiracy to cover up the abusive behavior in your family. The goal of recognizing what really happened is to hold your major caregivers accountable in your mind, so that you can separate the abuse from the precious child who experienced it. Holding caregivers accountable does not mean that you accuse them of anything. It just means owning your perception concerning what happened and getting in touch with the feeling reality that followed the less-than-nurturing events. . . . Blaming handcuffs you to the person who abused you and leaves you dependent upon that person's changing for you to have any recovery. This gives power to the offender and renders you, the victim, helpless—without the ability to protect yourself or change. Blaming will probably keep you stuck in the disease [codependency] and is likely to make it even worse.

Accountability means that you acknowledge what happened and who did it, but that you can do what you need to do to protect yourself and make the changes necessary to recover from the abuse of your past.[8]

— Pia Mellody

NINE

DEALT ANOTHER DIRTY CARD

I was making plans to pay Dad a surprise visit out in Georgia when cruel fate stepped in and dealt me a dirty card off the bottom of her deck.

In January of 1980, Dad had to go back into the hospital for an unexpected surgery on his right ankle and foot. It seemed that he had developed type 2 adult diabetes and this started a problem with blood thickening up and becoming sluggish passing through the plastic tubing. Something had to be done.

When the test results came back, they were not good. Gangrene was in his right foot. The only way to correct the problem was to amputate the foot at the ankle. He said the surgery was going to be a breeze and that he was expected to have a good recovery. Eventually, he would be fitted with a prosthetic foot and in a few months should be up dancing again. He told me not to worry, that he'd call me as soon after surgery as possible, which he did.

April 6, 1980: Dad was back in the hospital—this time to examine the stump and determine if he was ready for the prosthesis. He had called to let me know what was going on and said that he had gotten two separate complete physicals. Apart from the foot problem, he was in very good shape. Later that day Dad called. He said he was feeling kind of rocky. But other than that he seemed to be okay. We talked for a while, finally said good-bye, and hung up.

AN EARLY MORNING CALL

The next day, April 7th, two days after my birthday, at 5:30 in the morning, I was awakened by the phone. I picked up the receiver while still half asleep and tried to say hello. My words were garbled at best. Finally, I heard a voice asking me a whole bank of questions, half of which in my semi-sleep moment, I couldn't even understand. But the words, "I'm calling about your father," woke me up! In a few sentences, I was told that my father had just passed away. I came unglued and exploded.

I proceeded to tell the guy on the other end of the phone just what I thought of him waking me up at 5:30 in the morning and pulling this kind of sick joke on me. I slammed down the phone, laid back down, and tried to go back to sleep. Just as I was closing my eyes, the phone rang again. For some weird unexplainable reason, this time the ringing of the phone sounded like the bells of doom. I carefully picked up the phone and said, "Hello." Again, the same man's voice was on the other end. First thing he said was, "Mr. Rice, This is NOT a joke. This is serious. I need to speak with you about your father. Please do not hang up." The crispness and formality of the way he was speaking sent an icy chill down my back.

NOW I WAS AWAKE!

The man identified himself as the Patient Administrator of Martin Army Hospital, Fort Benning, Georgia. He said he was very sorry to be waking me up at such an ungodly hour but unfortunately that was the bad side of his job.

Before he went any further, he needed to ask me some questions to make positive identification to make sure he was indeed talking to the right Charles Rice. He must have asked me some thirty odd questions, and I answered them all. Then he explained what had happened to my father. He'd unexpectedly taken a turn for the worse the day before and his health rapidly slid downhill. Despite their best efforts, they were unable to save my dad. I was heartbroken.

I was asked to come as soon as possible. There was lots of paperwork for me to fill out and for the gentleman on the other end to finish up. I jotted down his name and phone number and promised to call back soon. He told me to please hurry. I said good-bye. My day—and the rest of my life—was off to a really rotten start.

The next morning I let the man know that I had borrowed some money and would be hopping on the next flight out. Approximately eighteen hours later, I was in Columbus. I was met at the airport by my father's lady friend, Amy, and a military chaplain. We exchanged rather tense greetings. A thunderstorm filled the sky as we drove to my father's house.

Next surprise—I had to call the police. My father's house had been broken into. Things just would not stop going wrong. After the police left, the three of us sat and talked for about an hour. The two of them left saying they'd be back the next morning at ten o'clock.

I was alone in my father's house and I felt like I was at home, the kind of home that until now I had never really had—not ever. Even though I was in my second marriage and had experienced two different homes with two different wives, I had never felt "at home." It was in this place, in my father's house, where at last I felt like I was truly home. That feeling is still hard to explain. I went to bed and slept well in my father's house.

I FELT SO CHEATED

Just as promised, at ten in the morning, the chaplain and Amy were at the door. The first stop was breakfast at the military's expense. Over bacon, eggs, and coffee, the three of us talked and got a little better acquainted. After breakfast, we headed to Fort Benning where I was taken to the base commander's office and things went on from there. As the day progressed, I was taken to the paymaster's office and discovered two checks were waiting for me: a military beneficiary check and another one from my father's private insurance company.

Our next stop was the mortuary where my father's body was being held. Once there, I was escorted into where Dad was. It was so hard to walk up to that casket. For the first time since I was five years old, I was going to get to see my father—and he was dead. Once at the casket, my knees buckled under me. I began to cry uncontrollably. The first time I get to see my dad and he's in a damned casket. Then from somewhere, a fierce burning rage boiled up in me. It boiled and churned. Then it exploded like Mt. Saint Helens. I wanted to hurt someone. I wanted to mangle someone. I wanted to hit; I wanted to swear; and I wanted to kill. The one person who had meant the most to me had been stolen from me a second time. The first time was when my parents had separated, and now when he was gone for good.

I was scared. I was frightened. I was alone. I wanted my father. Just when I was preparing to surprise him with a visit all the way from Oregon, this is the way I had to see him. I felt like some dark sinister person was lurking in the shadows, and I wanted his head on a silver platter. I felt so cheated. Someone was going to pay.

Suddenly, I let out a long guttural growl that turned into a frenzied calling howl like a wolf. When it passed, I was surrounded by people I wasn't even aware of until after this weird, grief-induced frenzy had passed. When I began to regain my strength of mind, the chaplain came up to me, put his arm around me, took me off to the side and helped me regain a sense of composure.

EXPRESSING GRIEF

Powerful, unexpected emotions can accompany grief. One cannot, with accuracy, predict how those feelings will gush out when we learn of the sudden loss of a loved one. In this case, there is historical evidence to consider that anger would be the learned response to life's troubles. After all, the example Charles grew accustomed to early on was his mother's graphic misuse of anger and his complete lack of power to do anything about it.

Recognize that children most often *catch* more of what they see acted out than what they hear. That is why we can surmise a learned reactive pattern, to a significant degree, settles into the child's life whether consciously or subconsciously. In a time of utter despair, with no way to change what had happened, Charles erupted like a volcano under pressure—just like his mother so often did.

Abuse victims should take a serious look at behavior patterns that were modeled in childhood. Unless there is an awareness of these potholes, they'll often be replicated. Do some role-playing before something traumatic comes upon you. Create a game plan that will allow you to respond appropriately rather than react negatively.

PAYING RESPECTS

If you are familiar with Star Trek: The Next Generation, you will see Worf do the same thing I did when one of his Klingon comrades dies.

After the viewing, I was taken back to my dad's house and told I would be picked up the next morning by the chaplain and some others precisely at 9 a.m.

Amy came back around five o'clock and we went to a place called Country's Bar-B-Q where I learned about real southern cooking. The chicken and ribs were awesome. I have never tasted anything like it since.

After dinner we went back to my father's house where we brought out Dad's photo albums. I saw pictures taken over the last fifteen years of his life. The pictures allowed me to see still another side of my dad I didn't know.

The next day the military showed up. Boy did they show up! A military limousine pulled into the driveway, and a full-sized bus like a super coach pulled up on the street side. Next thing I knew, a full military color guard silently filed out of the bus and formed a rank from the limo to the front door. All of them in uniforms so crisp and sharp I don't know how they got into them. Rifles at port arms, the two in the lead were carrying flagpoles, one with the American flag and the other with a Fort Benning flag with a cross on it. We all left the front door and went to the limo, with the color guard falling into step behind. Once we were in the limo, the color guard got back on the bus and we drove to the graveyard for the funeral service. There I met people from four square dance clubs and about a hundred more of my dad's friends and coworkers who came to pay respects to a man they had admired. After about forty-five minutes, the service started.

The entire service took about an hour or so. I held up pretty well all the way through the whole thing until the flag from my dad's casket was placed in my hands. Then a big rush like a tidal wave swept over me and I couldn't hold it back. I started crying like Niagara Falls. Then I heard that damned trumpeter off to the side as he began to play Taps. My crying intensified. I couldn't control it. I felt like I was being run through a shredder. I hurt beyond any understanding. Finally, the service was over and everyone left. A few stragglers hung around to talk to me. Finally, Amy took me back to the house, dropped me off, and said she'd keep in touch.

I spent four more days there before heading home. There were a lot of long, long miles and very little sleep in between. A week later, my wife and I packed up and moved to Georgia. We remained there until 1983 when I sold the house and once again returned to Medford, Oregon.

BACK IN OREGON

After returning to Oregon, things didn't go so well either. Soon my second wife developed kidney problems and had to go on dialysis. About a year later, her condition was detrimentally affecting our marriage. Just about the same time as our divorce was starting, she passed away from complications from the kidney *dialysis. From there I lost touch with reality. I started getting in trouble with the law, and yeah, I served time in jail a number of times. Nothing was major. It was all petty stuff, but I want you to know up front, I'm no angel, and I'm not perfect. I still have times that I get angry and lose my temper, but it is nowhere as bad as it used to be.*

My mother lived in Shady Cove, Oregon. I had tried at least ten times in the last fifteen years to bridge the gap between us. Finally, in 2004, I totally gave up trying to fill in the Grand Canyon between us. My mother still called me a no-good long-haired hippie. She never liked my long hair and mustache. But what's so crazily funny is that even though my mother called me a long-haired hippie, my mother absolutely would not have known a hippie if she was sitting in a java house surrounded by three hundred hippies all drinking coffee and listening to Dave Brubeck, Cal Tjader, and Charlie Byrd on the Wurlitzer jukebox.

I worked in the care-giving business for four years and saw enough of Alzheimer's, dementia, and senility to be confident that her mind was starting to take a big vacation from her. That was another reason I quit trying to establish some form of understanding between us. To my mother, I'll always be a no-good long-haired hippie and many, many other derogatory insulting filthy dirty names that no parent should ever call any child. She is stubborn, belligerent, bullheaded, cynical, self-centered, and egotistical.

I finally wised up and discovered that I was not only wasting my time trying, but I was also the only one beating my head on the wall looking for something salvageable with a woman who didn't care.

DEEP LONGINGS FOR LOVE

To be human is to experience close relationships. God wired us that way. The most important bond on earth is that of mother and child. When that relationship seems hopeless, the child suffers great hardship. In a way, it seems there's an invisible force that ties one to the other and the child's heartache follows him year after year, decade after decade. Behind the pain, where only deep longings can live, the desire to be loved doesn't want to give up. What wasn't received in childhood is still being chased after. There's a foraging for love, a hunger that needs to be fed by that parent, for as long as the child lives.

LIFE GOES ON

So now, I have a wonderful lady in my life that I adore, and we spend a lot of time together. I am now back to work after undergoing a major kidney cancer surgery in August 2006 and a major hernia surgery in March 2007. But for the last six or seven years, I have been running TV cameras for Public Broadcasting TV here in Medford and for Southern Oregon University's Rogue Valley public access TV. I've managed a twin-screen drive-in theater, been in two movies, and am now very happily volunteering as a camera operator for KBLN Better Life TV in Grants Pass Oregon. They are a wonderful bunch of sincere, caring, and loving people. I'm really glad to be there and feel that I am being made into a much better person just by being a part of what KBLN is doing and helping in my own little way to do the Lord's work. The rest of the time, you can find me out on most any roadside in Jackson or Josephine County in hot, cold, or soaking wet weather in construction zones flagging traffic and trying to keep drivers slowed down and construction workers as safe as possible.

The tragic finale to this whole story is that, although up until 1980 both my parents were alive, it has been horribly difficult to grow old and still have no father to go fishing with or to go kite-flying or all the other things that small boys do with their fathers.

Then to have to grow up with a mother that hates you with every fiber of her being and be subjected to her continual verbal, emotional, and—worst of all—her extreme raging out of control hatred and volcanic anger and the resultant physical beatings that went on without end was at the least perpetually emotionally scaring. You may ask what was the reason for these lifelong beatings that I did not cause, ask for, want or deserve? It was all because my mother seemed to have a genuine hatred for my father for some unexplainable reason, and even though they divorced when I was five years old, she carried, this illogical hatred over and inflicted all that hatred against her own son. As the years progressed, she became worse with every passing day.

Yes, I often see myself as a defective person. I have felt like an orphaned child since I was five years old. I pray I will recover from this. Otherwise, I will probably carry this heaviness to my grave, where thankfully it will finally come to an end.

A DAMAGED SENSE OF SELF

How sad it is to read of a mother who causes her son to feel he's both defective and an orphan. Destructive parenting year after year had heaped hurt upon hurt. Raw honesty is communicated from the depths of a broken heart.

Be assured that God did not approve of this mother's behaviors nor does God see Charles, or you, as defective. God looks upon Charles Rice, and you and me, as His precious children, created in His own image. No defects. Dive head deep into this truth! Soak in its reality. Embrace your Father in Heaven. Hold tight to the never-ending love He has for you. No longer believe the venomous lies of the abuser.

Isaiah 57:20–21 helps us know what God says about wicked people who sling mud on others: *"The wicked are like the tossing sea, which cannot rest, whose waves cast up mire and mud. 'There is no peace,' says my God, 'for the wicked.'"*

A sweet measure of comfort is found in knowing the wicked will not find peace. The rest of us, if we're willing, can set about finding God's peace. Isn't that what we search for? Peace comes when we resolutely release the abuser into our Heavenly Father's care. We lay down that heavy burden and free up space to think of better things.

I'M DONE

I have tried a couple of times to get counseling help with this, but so far all the counselors have really done is say, "You're an adult now. Grow up and get over it." They want to classify me as a depressed person and try to put me on their dumb happy pills. Those things don't solve the deep-rooted problem. I just quit seeing those counselors. As far as I could see, there was no reason to give them my hard-earned money.

You may think that even something as small as hearing "Taps" at a military funeral is no big deal. You're wrong. If I even so much as hear "Taps" on a newscast or anywhere else, I completely fall apart and start crying. I have to shut off the volume the second I hear it or else I'm done in. That's how much I miss my father.

Since divorcing my father, my mother has married and divorced about five times. Her last husband, Gene, died from alcoholism. Alcoholism that she started him on because my mother was and possibly still is an incredibly heavy drinker. So see, my mother has ruined a lot of other peoples' lives too. And believe it or not, she has never taken one iota of responsibility for any of these ruined lives. She always said it was the other person's fault.

So, I can only say this to my mother: "Josephine, in Shady Cove, Oregon, I, your son, Charles Rice, have given up claiming you as my mother. As far as I am concerned, you are dead and gone. You, and your actions over all these years, have caused an equal and opposite reaction from me: You're dead and gone; you have vanished without a trace, no funeral, no tears, no flowers, no NOTHING!!!

"I still struggle on with the problems you made many years ago. I hope you are extremely proud of your accomplishments. You really left your mark in life. Will I ever find peace and closure? I don't know. I just don't know. Right now, I see myself as the damaged orphan."

THE PAIN OF UTTER LONELINESS

Pain big enough to denounce another human being is serious deep pain. To Charles, the longing to receive love from his mother felt unattainable. He gave up.

To feel like an orphan is a very lonely statement to make. While Charles's experience with counselors didn't work out, don't believe help can't be found. There are effective counselors, and various other organizations that specialize in providing services to hurting people, who can genuinely help to move you beyond the hurt of abuse. Search out support groups in your community. You are not alone.

If you are ready...

Reach for Fresh Joy *[for the abused]*

> "'For in him we live and move
> and have our being.'
> As some of your own poets have said,
> 'We are his offspring.'"
> Acts 17:28

Grief is a deep-seated emotion. Grief hurts our hearts.

If you have suffered the loss of someone close to you, what was your initial reaction? _____
_____

Are you angry at God? _____

What would you like to say to God?
_____
_____

Do you feel like an orphan? _____

What has made you feel that way?
_____
_____

> God is the Father who will never leave
> or forsake you. "As I was with Moses, so I will be with you;
> I will never leave you nor forsake you"
> Joshua 1:5

How does this promise from scripture make you feel?
_____
_____
_____

> "Though my father and mother forsake me,
> the LORD will receive me."
> Psalm 27:10

Sit quietly before the Lord and let this beautiful and precious promise settle into your heart and mind. Write down any reflective thoughts you might want to remember:
_____
_____
_____
_____

If you are ready...

Reach for Fresh Hope *[for the abuser]*

"Because of the LORD's great love we are not consumed,
for his compassions never fail."
Lamentations 3:22

Love and compassion personify the heart of God. Because people are made in God's image, we are created to give love and act with compassion. When that doesn't happen, relationships suffer. Compassion means having mercy, showing tenderness, and caring about the afflictions of others.

Would you call yourself a compassionate person? _____

Why?
_____
_____
_____

Recall a time when you treated your child with compassion:
_____
_____
_____
_____

Does your son or daughter know you love him/her? _____
Or, does that child believe you hate him/her? _____

Why would that be true?
_____
_____

Abuse and compassion cannot coexist. They are opposing forces. A child who is abused will have a hard time believing he/she is worthy of love. Like Charles Rice, your child might feel like an orphan, too. What can you do to begin to repair the damage you've inflicted?

_____
_____
_____

Will you begin to take great delight in your child? _____

What might happen if you did?

_____
_____
_____
_____

> "Blessed is the one whom God corrects;
> so do not despise the discipline of the Almighty."
> Job 5:17

You were born with an inherent sense of goodness, strength, and wisdom that you should be able to call upon in moments of self doubt. Unfortunately, you may have lost touch with this inner sense because of the way you were raised and by the messages you received to the contrary.[9]

— Beverly Engel

TEN

SURPRISED!

Years passed. The 2009 calendar had been hung on the wall.

My relationship with Mary was a distant memory—having ended after eight years. Two more marriages collapsed. I am now with Rachel.

Tuesday morning, January 27, 2009 started out in an ordinary way. Rachel and I were enjoying a calm morning. Breakfast was being made when, at ten past nine, the phone rang. Rachel answered. After a few words, she passed the phone off to me.

Naturally, I said, "Hello."

A gruff voice on the other end asked, "Is this Charles Rice?"

Immediately I froze. How quickly I recognized the voice on the other end. It took me about ten seconds to find my voice. With full guard up, I cautiously answered, "Yes, it is."

The woman on the other end said, "This is your mother."

She was so matter of fact that all I could say was, "Yes, I know it is." I was thinking, *after more than fifty years you're finally realizing and admitting it!*

Then she said, "If you could and would, I need your help."

After all the years of fights, problems, and more fights and more problems with my mother, here she is now asking for my help.

With great caution and emotions kept in check, I asked, "What is it you need?"

She started crying profusely. It took some time for her to regain her composure. While she was crying, I put the phone on speaker mode so Rachel could listen, too.

My mother finally got it out that for the last two years she had been living in an assisted living facility in Eagle Point, Oregon. She was now having trouble with the administrator and the other powers that be in that place. It seemed she had caused some kind of disturbance in the living center and was being evicted. They were giving her just forty-eight hours to move out!

"What do you want me to do?" I asked.

"Do you know of anywhere that might be available to rent that I could move into immediately?"

At that time, I wasn't aware of any available places and told her she'd have to go through the newspaper and rental agencies. She started to yell at me that she didn't have the time to go through the newspaper or the rental agencies, that she couldn't see that well anymore because she had glaucoma in both eyes and was legally blind.

As nice as possible I reminded her of what she had told me the last time I tried to contact her, back in 2006, looking for any family history of cancer. I told her how she'd screamed and yelled at me, called me names, and threatened to call the police on me for disturbing the peace and other whacko threats she was throwing around. My doctor needed the information because I was battling kidney cancer at the time. She expressed no empathy. My mother went so far as to have the Shady Cove police call me and put me through the third and fourth degree over the phone.

After I reminded her of that incident, she started crying again. Rachel and I listened to her cry for another five minutes until she regained her composure.

"I guess I deserve everything you said, and I am sorry for causing you problems."

Now that REALLY blew me out of the water! That was the very first time I had ever heard my mother apologize and say she was sorry for anything!

RESPOND SLOWLY

Surprised was an understatement. She needed him? The thought of such a thing was blowing his mind.

Can you relate to Charles's apprehension?

After all the years, his mother's voice still held a dark power to instantly set him on edge. Try to imagine the landslide of mixed emotions that assailed him in that moment. The fear, the hope, the apprehension, the distrust, the contempt, and yet a desperate longing for the child in him to be loved by his mother; the same woman who had treated him so badly. How confusing to have so many emotions swirling around at the same time.

When a mother's relationship with her child is chronicled by painful experiences, there will likely be a breach as wide as the Grand Canyon. Doubts and a hesitancy to get too close are smart thoughts to heed. You should be guarded.

Charles was wise to respond slowly—to briefly collect his thoughts—before answering. The whole conversation had come at him without warning. How wide should he open the door to his heart this time?

I AGREED TO HELP

We talked a little longer. I remembered one place: a studio apartment that had just been vacated two days earlier in the same complex where we had lived for the past ten years. Mother then gave me her address and phone number and asked if I would inquire about that apartment and call her back. So, I did. Our manager said the apartment wasn't prepped for a new tenant yet. After explaining the need and that it was for my eighty-seven-year-old mother, they agreed to get the janitorial crew to work on it and have the apartment ready the next day.

When I called my mother, she cried and thanked me over and over for almost ten minutes. Next we were asked to come out to where she lived to sit down and talk. This also caught me way off balance. She wasn't in the habit of asking me over. In fact, quite the opposite was the norm: Stay away!

I agreed to the visit. Eagle Point was only thirty minutes away. As we entered the room, the person I saw was not the woman I remembered. This woman looked frail, hunched over, a white-haired old woman. What I didn't notice at first was her stooped stance as she leaned on a red and white cane. If she had stood up straight, she would have been a good six feet tall. Mother walked up to me, gave me a hug, and said it was really nice to see me.

All the niceness was just too much for me. No way was this behavior my mother's normal! I had no idea how to act or react.

We sat down. Slowly, a real conversation started. Soon we learned that she was recovering from hip surgery and even though she was legally blind and couldn't see you at all if you were right in front of her, she could see you just fine if you stood off to the side.

Before long we learned why she was being evicted. The nursing home employees insisted that she sit in the dining room at a table where a black man was seated across from her. Every time the staff tried to seat her at the table where this gentleman was at her assigned table, she went off in a loud tirade for half an hour disrupting all the residents. That scene happened three times a day. The administrator refused to work out another seating arrangement. Instead, he felt she was old enough to get over her ridiculous prejudices. Of course, all that did was make her even angrier. She blamed her prejudices against the African-American people on her upbringing.

INSECURE RELATIONSHIP STYLES

Charles showed compassion at a time when it might have been easier—even wiser—to hang up the phone. Three things might help us sort through why an abused son would risk caring.

1. He's got a tender heart for those in need.

2. He's still behaving as the small child who is trying to please his mother.

3. Hope. There is a deep longing for a mended relationship with his mother.

Dr. Tim Clinton and Dr. Gary Sibcy have this to say: "Our insecure relationship styles are designed to protect us from pain in our youth. But when these styles are played out in our adult relationships, they can cause more pain, unnecessary pain. The repair process involves breaking the vicious cycle."[10]

Children seldom give up hope despite maltreatment—even after they are grown. That is one of the deepest mysteries of the human heart. The only way to make sense of this phenomenon is to realize that from the moment a baby emerges from the womb, there is a deep-seated need to be loved and accepted—especially from a mother figure.

THE BIG MOVE

Money wasn't an issue. Mother had lots of money in her savings account. The next day we rented a U-Haul truck, loaded up all my mother's belongings, and got to the apartment by 4:15 that afternoon. Rachel and I worked hard unloading the truck and getting the place livable before nightfall.

A couple days later I took her to the bank and helped her transfer her account to a nearby local branch only a block from the apartment. I showed her how to go across the parking lot to the mailboxes and how to go the other direction to the big supermarket next door. I installed an outdoor electrical outlet so she could plug in her electric scooter, and I also put up a weatherproof tarp to park it under at night. Permission was given to paint in a regulation handicapped parking space in front of her apartment. So many other details, like telephone service and grocery shopping, were tended to.

Rachel and I were glad to do these things. Finally, she told us she was all settled in and happy to be away from the place she called, "The hell hole."

ONE WEEK LATER

Mother was getting bored listening to the radio all day. I told her that when she was ready we'd go to the cable TV office and get her hooked up.

There were about twenty people ahead of us and only three service reps were working the desk. We sat there almost an hour. Mother was getting grouchy. I told her to just hang on, that the reps were very busy and would get to us as soon as they could. Another thirty minutes went by before we got up to the counter. After answering many questions and filling in lots of forms, a receiver and remote were brought out. The rep started writing down serial and model numbers and the last thing she did was to ask for my mother's credit card.

Little did I know what was about to happen. I didn't see it coming.

"Why do you need a credit card?" Mother asked.

The rep explained they couldn't take cash. It was company policy.

"I've never had a credit card and you don't need one!" was Mother's reply. "You can have plain cash or go straight to hell!" she shouted.

I tried to intervene but it was too late. My mother reached into her purse and pulled out a big wad of money and threw it in the air at the rep. "Here's the money. Take it and put it on the bill and do your f***ing job!"

Once more the rep calmly repeated company policy while my mother's commotion went on and on until she stormed to the door! This whole scene lasted about eight minutes, but within that short span of time my dear mother had raised such a commotion that even the other people waiting behind us left the building. I stayed just long enough to pick up the money and to apologize for what had happened.

In counting the money, I discovered $760 in $20 bills. Upon getting back in the car, I handed the money to my mother. She screamed at me that she didn't want it. I let the subject drop. Somehow, as we travelled back across town, I was able to sneak all the money back into her purse without her catching on.

After she had calmed down a bit, I asked if she had a TV somewhere. The answer was, "No. Why get a TV when I can't get service?"

I assured her there were other options for TV service that we hadn't tried yet. At that, she agreed to go shopping for a television. She finally settled on a forty-inch flat screen model. Mother paid cash for it; no problem at all.

The next day we drove to talk with Yvonne, the lady who had done the paperwork for the satellite TV service Rachel and I have. All was well until the subject of credit cards came up. Mother was starting up again with the temper tantrum. Oh boy!!!

Immediately, I got her up, out the door, and in the car. I stepped back into the office long enough to apologize to Yvonne, ask her if she could work something else out, and to tell her I'd be back in a few minutes. I headed back to mother's place and dropped her off with words to get her temper under control.

Yvonne had the paperwork ready when I returned. She'd even made an appointment to have mother's service hooked up and running the next day. What she'd done was to make her service an extension of ours. And there would be no charge to hook it up.

Back in the car I felt like some kind of comic book superhero. With my mother out of the way, everything had gone click, click, click and what needed to be done was quickly accomplished.

The next day went right from morning until night. I was able to locate a brand new bathtub shower bench (at no cost) and find a safety grab handle, too. No problem. Soon I had a 370-pound capacity safety grab rail for her shower wall and the rental agency's permission to install. The satellite dish for the TV service went just as smoothly. Within minutes of the installer's arrival, she was watching television.

I was feeling pretty proud of myself. To make things even better, by the end of that day, my mother had examined my handiwork and declared it, "Perfect!"

Those words had been a long time coming. But they sure felt good.

GIFTS OF AFFIRMATION

Angry outbursts aside, Charles managed to keep a handle on things, and in spite of his mother's violent history, he worked hard to make Mother's apartment comfortable and safe. At this point in the story Charles was feeling great, like a superhero. A sense of pride popped up in his tone and he felt his worth as a human being buoyed when his mother pronounced his work, "Perfect." That was an over-the-moon, dream-come-true moment.

Sometimes our Heavenly Father pours out gifts of affirmation so old wounds can heal. Often these blessings come from unexpected sources and deliver a much-needed emotional boost in the nick of time. At this point in the telling of Charles's story, it's believable that God put those positive words on his mother's heart, and in her mouth, specifically for his benefit. Charles had spent a lifetime desperately needing to hear his mother's appreciation. Never had he imagined such a compliment would escape her lips. But oh, how his heart swelled when it did.

It is not unusual that those subjected to child abuse are also codependent people. Their happiness is determined in great part by outside stimulus—by what other people say.

John Bradshaw, in his book, *Healing the Shame That Binds You*, says: "Much has been written about co-dependency. All agree that it is about the loss of selfhood. Co-dependency is a condition wherein one has no inner life. Happiness is on the outside. Good feelings and self-validation lie on the outside. They can never be generated from within. . . . It is my belief that internalized shame is the essence of co-dependency.[11]

Charles had an unmistakable lift to his emotions upon hearing his mother speak words of affirmation.

BRINGING EBBY HOME

The next day Rachel and I noticed something in Mother's voice that made me ask what was wrong. She'd been thinking about Ebby (Ebony), her cat, who was living at C.A.T.S., a cat shelter where no cat is ever put down. Until then, we didn't know she had a cat.

"Do you want me to get Ebby back?"

"You want to go get Ebby right now?" she asked.

"You miss your cat, so why sit here moping about missing your cat when we can go get him and bring him home. Stop fretting."

In a flash, Mother was up and headed for the door. We bought a litter box, litter, and cat food on our way to the shelter. Upon walking through the front door we were met by a huge fluffy, jet black cat stretched out on the counter. My mother immediately said, "That's Ebby!"

After a few words with the people at the shelter, we headed home with one big black cat. Back at her apartment, we let him explore while we put the litter box and food and in place. He ate his fill, and drank, and hopped up on Mother's lap. Good grief! You could hear Ebby purr from twenty feet away! He knew he was home again. And Mother was beaming like a 1,000-watt lightbulb. With that, Rachel and I took our leave and went home.

I felt happy all over, like I'd made a small impression on my mother. Because of my ability to help, she had her cat back for companionship and wasn't so alone anymore.

Rachel and I set about doing all we could to make Mother feel welcome in our apartment and an integral part of our lives. I'm really amazed at how nicely things are going between my mother and me.

If you are ready...

Reach for Fresh Joy *[for the abused]*

"Therefore my heart is glad and
my tongue rejoices; my body also will rest secure."
Psalm 16:9

What might it mean for your heart to be glad?
_____

Name some of the "good" things Charles did for his mother:
_____
_____

What do you think prompted such kindness?
_____
_____

Have you ever experienced a time of doing good and feeling happy because of words your abuser spoke? _____
Recall the "good" you have done:
_____
_____

Write down your abuser's words of appreciation:
_____
_____
_____

How did those words make you feel?
_____
_____
_____

What might it mean for one's tongue to rejoice?
_____
_____
_____

How might it feel for your body to rest secure?
_____
_____
_____

Are you able to rest secure? _____
What has allowed that to happen?
_____
_____

If you are unable to rest secure right now, what do you believe is keeping you from that rest?
_____
_____

Take a minute to be still. Ask the Lord to help you rest secure. He is your sure resting place.

If you are ready...

Reach for Fresh Hope *[for the abuser]*

"Does not the ear test words as the tongue tastes food?"
Job 12:11

There's been a change of heart between Charles Rice and his mother. What brought that change about?
_____
_____

What would it take for you to seek help from a son or daughter?
_____
_____

Do you think your child would come to your aid? _____
Why would you think that?
_____
_____

Consider speaking words of praise or appreciation to your child. What would you say?
_____
_____

How might those words make him/her feel?
_____
_____

How does speaking good words make you feel?
_____
_____
_____
_____
_____

> "The lips of the righteous nourish many."
> Proverbs 10:21

A key to developing your children's self-esteem is acknowledging their self-worth. Self-worth refers to things we have come to believe about our importance and value. If children don't have feelings of self-worth, they're less resilient in facing adversity, and they have trouble solving problems out in the world. Effectively helping your children develop their self-worth demands that you help them maximize all their distinctive gifts and qualities—and let them know that they do matter in their family and in society.[12]

— Dr. Phil McGraw

ELEVEN
Truth and Generosity

During the first year, Mother and I talked a lot and did a lot of catching up about things from the past that needed to be settled. I took her to doctor appointments, the hair salon, and the V.A. Domiciliary for medical needs and a variety of other veterans' functions she regularly attended. Mother told me a whole lot about her past that, until then, I knew absolutely nothing about.

Some things were a surprise and others hard to believe. She said that when she was about ten years old she and her sister (What! She had a sister?) were put up for adoption by their mother. As the story went, she was adopted by a family named Faulkner in Ft. Wayne, Indiana. It seems this Faulkner family had a family member who was a mogul who was apparently quite well to do and owned a newspaper and a couple publishing firms in the Ft. Wayne and Chicago area back in the 1920–30s. If I ever do a family history search, I'll probably have to search for the Faulkners to know if what she has revealed is actually true. At one telling the family was in Ft. Wayne and at another time she'd say Chicago. Who knows? Maybe they had two homes.

During Mother's first year in the new apartment, Rachel and I started noticing early signs of senility or dementia. Once in a while she'd forget that she had to use the remote to change TV channels and was trying to find the channel knob on the TV when there wasn't one. Or, she would be looking for the key to lock the front door from the inside or putting her thermostat clear up to ninety degrees. She'd give answers or make a remark that made absolutely no sense whatsoever; say something one way and within minutes say the same thing totally different. A couple times I found her having trouble just counting money, and it wasn't due to her vision problems. Things like counting two $10 bills as $20s. When we brought this to her attention, she would get mad and vehemently deny she'd done anything like what we'd told her had happened. She'd claim we were trying to confuse her. Because of this, we did have our little ups and downs.

Overall, things weren't bad.

On appointment days she'd have me stop at one of the local burger or chicken joints for a bite of lunch or dinner. She'd always insist on getting something for Rachel and me, too. This happened three or four times a month. Mother bought it all.

She even made me her personal caregiver and paid me $300 a month to check on her every day, vacuum the carpet, take out the trash, bring in her mail, and whatever other trivial things she needed done. Many times I told her I didn't need to be paid—but she insisted. It was easier to quit arguing and let her pay me. She had no shortage of money. Her V.A. benefits, teacher's retirement, and a couple of other things put a little more than $4,500 a month in her bank account.

SURPRISED BY GENEROSITY

During the start of the second year, my mother absolutely shocked us both with her generosity. She'd already asked when Rachel's birthday was and of course knew mine. What we didn't see coming was when she sat us both down.

"Is there anything you've seriously wanted to buy?" she asked.

Rachel mentioned the only thing we were trying to save for was a computer for me and a laptop for her. She wanted to know if we had set any money aside to get these things.

"We've just started saving and have $150 socked away," I answered. "The one I settled on sells for $2,600 and Rachel's laptop is priced at $600."

One thing that struck my mother funny was that Rachel's birthday was February 13th, and that Valentine's Day was the very next day. Our jaws hit the floor when Mother told us to go ahead and get our computers and make sure we got the correct total price. She'd pay for everything and didn't expect them to be cheap. We began to protest—but the more we protested, the more she insisted. She wouldn't stop pressing the matter until we agreed to go home and pull out the Dell catalog and get the price nailed down.

Sure enough, the computers cost $3,200. Mother didn't blink an eye. Instead, she got into her money stash and told me to count out the bills. Of course a cashier's check was needed to send off with the order to Dell. No problem. Mother also reasoned that if she needed something researched in the future, those computers would come in handy for her purposes, too.

The next two or three weeks went by nicely.

GOOD GIFTS

Generosity of this magnitude from this mother was a serious new twist. Giving good gifts with no strings attached is wonderful. It allows us to see another side of her. Those gifts could be interpreted as a tangible sign of acceptance and love. Or, the opposite can be true. Gifts from an abuser can sometimes be a cruel form of manipulation. Either way, the computers this couple longed to possess were suddenly within reach. Mother had asked the question and she put up the money.

Yes, this sounded totally out of character. But, at the same time, Charles received her generosity as a warm, long-overdue reason to believe his mother might really care about him and the desires of his heart, like a good mother would. The pricey gifts were accepted as objects of her approval. But was any of that true? Did she approve of him? Or was something more manipulative being acted out? It's good to weigh unseen motives carefully and not forget the abuser's track record too quickly.

SHOPPING TROUBLES

Then the weather turned wet and cold. Mom wanted some galoshes. The modern shoe stores didn't have the slip-over boots she wanted. They didn't even know what we were talking about! I thought everybody knew what those silly things were but I suppose that was true in days gone by. Even the catalogues didn't carry galoshes. We struck out on that shopping expedition. The Army surplus store didn't have a pair. Those who knew what we were trying to find hadn't seen a pair of galoshes in years.

Mother was fit to be tied. Rather than listening to her tirade and swearing, I took her back home, and then went to my place to search for galoshes on the computer. I found out the manufacturers had discontinued them back in the early 90s because people were getting trendy and there was no longer a market for galoshes.

My mother couldn't accept it even after I handed her the printouts to examine under her expander viewer that takes any page of any size print and can blow it up almost 250 times for people with vision problems. Her tantrum started again.

"Getting mad won't do any good," I said. "It could make your heart problem act up. There is no sense in getting totally bent out of shape over something we have no control over."

"I don't have a temper problem!" she said.

"Oh yes you do and it's much worse than mine," I rebutted. "I've learned to keep my temper under pretty good control."

But in my mother's case, she did have a bad heart condition. When she got upset, her heart would start galloping and the next thing you knew, she had to sit down and take a nitro pill. For the next few days she had pains in her chest and that scared me. I was just starting to get my mother back and I didn't want to lose her because of a stupid heart attack initiated by her raging temper.

I tried to keep the conversation light. That didn't work. She flew off to Mars in a monster fit—screamed and yelled until I thought she'd keel over. It was time for Rachel and me to leave. That ended a very bad day.

HE'S SCARED TO LOSE HER

Life is such a mixture of conflicting emotions. Often the abused still feel love for their abuser moms. Charles doesn't want his mother to die of a heart attack. Only a heart that loves could say that. Despite the troubles, there is a genuine thread of affection that runs from him to her.

EMBARRASSED

By April 2011, the Rogue Valley was boasting spring colors. Mother had lived across the lot from us for fifteen months. Things started to go further downhill. Right after payday Mother would ask me to take her shopping at Wal-Mart. She'd pull clothes off racks or shelves, look at them, mumble some words about the garments being nothing but crap, throw them on the floor, and walk on. She'd repeat this garbage in the woman's section at least fifteen times every time she'd go in there. She'd go rack to rack, shelf to shelf, and repeat this stunt of holding something up and then throwing it on the floor and walking on, just to do it again and again. I'd trail along behind her picking up the clothes and folding them or rehanging them and putting them back on the racks or shelves where they belonged.

Those behaviors did not line up with someone who was in control of her faculties. Other times she'd get very vocal with a clerk if the store didn't carry a particular item. I'd step in and try to explain how the stores can't possibly carry everything.

She'd turn on me and say, "You sure are a big know-it-all. You always have an answer for everything!"

I'd respond, "Things don't work like they did twenty years ago. You're out of touch with the real world."

She'd scream and yell at me right there in the store. That embarrassed the hell out of me. At that, I'd just shut my mouth and let her go on her merry way.

REALLY?—SHE CALLED ME A WHIZ KID!

Most days Rachel and I would arrive at Mother's place around four in the afternoon. The three of us would sit around and talk very animatedly about just about anything, making wisecracks and laughing like mad. One day in particular I was blown away by what my mother was saying. She was actually beaming with pride as she talked to Rachel, telling her what a whiz kid I used to be when I was in my teens. That was huge! Both because of what she said about me and because I was seeing how much she really liked Rachel. She had never liked any of my prior wives and did her best to insult and degrade them until they left. Now this was a big turnaround!

From what I had seen since that first phone call from her, I was beginning to feel that my mother was being genuine and honest about restarting our relationship. I didn't want to get my hopes up too high, too fast. I had done that before and each time those hopes got thrown over the cliff and smashed on the rocks below. It's not the fall that hurts—it's the sudden crashing stop at the bottom.

IS THIS DIVINE PROVIDENCE?

Call it fate, call it destiny, call it good things come to those who wait, call it divine providence, call it an act of God. Don't get me wrong. I wasn't questioning what had happened. I was having trouble understanding it. Like a reporter, I was trying to eke out the mystery of who, what, where, when, and why of a blockbuster exposé. The best I could do was accept what was happening and be glad that things were now the way they were instead of the way they had been since I was five years old. Not to overdo the movie talk, but this seemed like a movie where the pieces were coming together in a, "They all lived happily ever after," kind of way.

It was nice we could sit down and talk without pecking at each other and ruffling one another's feathers. As we talked that day, things slowly turned toward the past. She started the conversation by saying, "I am so fortunate to have you here with me so you can help me with my needs."

"Mom, I've tried so many times in the last twenty-five years to talk to you and every time you shut me out and snubbed me. If you only knew how much that hurt every time you did that."

Mom came over to me and hugged me and said she had finally realized she'd been blinded about me and had wronged her son.

I told her that there were times when I hurt beyond belief when she blocked me out. I felt so alone, abandoned, and unwanted all at the same time. I was feeling frustration and burning anger that made me want to grab her and shake her until I either slapped some sense into her or until she fell apart. Mom said she understood how I felt and that over all that time all the things she had been doing must have been ripping me apart inside.

I told her that it was so bad that physically, mentally, and emotionally, I was a total walking disaster. I told her how I couldn't even function at school, told her that I had only a very small circle of friends at school and that other than them, I was a loner everywhere I went. I told her I could only feel comfortable around those few friends because they also lived the same kind of hell and physical and emotional abuse that I did. Yes, birds of a feather had flocked together.

The story continued to pour out of me. I told of how the few friends of mine and our girlfriends would make plans at school *each week to meet at a prearranged place with all our weekend gear (tents, sleeping bags, food, drinks, soda pop, booze, cigarettes, and pot). We'd fuel up our cars and caravan to a predetermined beach location where we knew our parents would never find us. After school on Friday, all of us were ready to go so none of us had to go home for anything.*

I was quite detailed about what we had done on those beach jaunts. The combination of the beach, the seclusion, the unwinding, cooking our own food, drinking, smoking pot, and the sex we had with our girlfriends was the only stuff that helped us maintain some degree of sanity.

When we got together it was soothing, like taking medicine for a severe sickness. Only then did we feel safe enough to both give love and feel loved. The booze and pot had relaxed our minds and gave us a break from the emotional pain and anxiety. The eight of us were all messed-up, hurt, lost kids. Our running away weekends was like physical therapy. Without those escapes a few of us might have cracked up, jumped off a cliff somewhere, or maybe picked up a gun. Somehow, back then, we were smart enough to know when to run for the hills instead of showing up at a school and shooting the place up. We didn't try to stay around and wrestle with it. We ran away. For a couple days we had freedom from all the hell we lived with at home.

Mom said that she had really made a mess of things and that she was not much of a mother back then and that she was beginning to understand why I always acted the way I did. She added that she would get so furious when she couldn't find me on the weekends and she guessed that was why she always exploded at me on Sunday evenings when I came back home.

During the couple of hours we talked, a lot of ground was covered. More of the gap between us closed. I began to think that if things kept getting better, maybe one day I'd get brave enough to ask her to open up about my father. But that might mean opening a can of worms. I had no idea how she would react to that kind of talk.

REAL TALK

Real talk! What an encouraging conversation. Honesty. Admission of wrongs. Praise. Hurts were revealed, voices were calm, and candid pent-up feelings about the past were brought to the surface. In the end there was empathy from mother to son. This is how healing begins for the abused and the abuser. Both have to get real talk in motion and keep emotions in check. Call it being open. Call it being vulnerable. Pride takes a holiday as dirty laundry is aired. The results are better understanding and a release of tension.

Charles began to feel the rift between them had perhaps started to close.

If you are ready...

Reach for Fresh Joy *[for the abused]*

"Instead, we will speak the truth in love,
growing in every way more and more like Christ."
Ephesians 4:15 NLT

It takes courage to speak truth. But truth opens the door to understanding and promotes healing of relationships.

How did Charles begin this conversation with his mother? Was it with a gentle spirit or an angry accusing tone?_____
_____

How did his mother react?
_____
_____
_____

What, from Ephesians 4:15, is the key ingredient when having a heart-to-heart talk?
_____
_____
_____

Why is it important for love to be present?
_____
_____

Take a minute to remember a time when you had a "truth" talk with your abuser. What was your attitude when the conversation began? _____

Who initiated the discussion? _____

How did the other person respond?
_____
_____
_____

In what way did that talk become a positive or negative experience?
_____
_____
_____

If you have not yet had that heart-to-heart talk with your abuser about the abuse and how it affected you, what can be done to open up an honest dialogue?
_____
_____
_____
_____
_____

If you are ready...

Reach for Fresh Hope *[for the abuser]*

"From the fruit of their lips people are filled with good things,
and the work of their hands brings them reward."
Proverbs 12:14

Has there been a time when you confessed to being a poor parent? _____

How did your child react?
_____
_____

What brought you to that moment of honesty?
_____
_____

If you have not taken that step, will you go to your child and admit your wrongs? _____
When? _____

How will you open that conversation?
_____
_____

Will you invite your son or daughter to have a "truth" talk with you? _____
When? _____

What will help you be a good listener to what your child might say during the "truth" talk?

_____

_____

_____

How has the start of a renewed relationship with your son or daughter made you feel?

____ Happy   ____ Worried   ____ Confused
____ Indifferent   ____ Blessed   ____ Loved

> "Instead, we will speak the truth in love,
> growing in every way more and more like Christ."
> Ephesians 4:15 NLT

Speaking the truth in love means saying what's on your mind in a way that demonstrates respect, promotes better understanding, and honors Jesus.

I push people very hard to confront toxic parents. I do this for one simple reason: confrontation works. Through the years I've seen confrontations make dramatic, positive changes in the lives of thousands of people. This doesn't mean I don't appreciate how frightened people feel when they even think about confronting their parents. The emotional stakes are high. But the mere fact that you're doing it, that you're facing what are probably some of your deepest fears, is enough to begin to change the balance of power between you and your parents. . . . The alternative to confrontation is to live with these fears. If you avoid taking positive action on your own behalf, you're reinforcing your feelings of helplessness and inadequacy, you're undermining your self-respect. What you don't hand back, you pass on. If you don't deal with your fear, your guilt, and your anger at your parents, you're going to take it out on your partner or your children.[13]

— Dr. Susan Forward

TWELVE

SHATTERED DREAMS

I should have seen the warning signs. But I didn't catch on soon enough. Perhaps deep down inside there was such a desperate desire for this relationship to be what I had always hoped it could be, that I ignored what was right before my eyes. Mother's irrational outbursts showed up at unexpected times. Now she was targeting her old place of residence, the assisted living center. She kept writing letters of complaint making hair-brained claims of every sort from the types of food being served to how the food was being served to that same black gentleman she used to complain about when she did live there and how he was supposedly still causing problems for the other residents.

Come to find out she was getting inside information from a ninety-seven-year-old woman at the facility who would call her five or six times a day with all kinds of tall tales. That's all it took for Mother to write nasty letters to the corporate offices, the senior services agency, the Attorney General, and last but not least, the Oregon State Board of Nursing! Oh yes, she got replies to all her letters. Every one of them briefly stated the same thing: The complaints were investigated and deemed to be unfounded.

When I asked her why she kept causing trouble for them she said she intended to continue until she succeeded in closing their doors for good. Rachel told Mother she was wasting her time and my mother got mad and started yelling that she was not wasting her time because she had nothing but time on her hands. She was going to continue her campaign of trouble against that place. With that situation brewing, and that kind of mind-set, we took our leave.

During this same period of time my mother started having problems with falls. Most were blamed on stumbling over her seventeen-pound cat or tripping over the extension cord that came from under her bed over to the electric recliner. She knew the cord was there and that there was an oversized throw rug covering the cord. Still she said she tripped over it.

Upon inspecting the rug and cord, neither had been moved from their original place.

We believed she had become fall prone. After the falls, she'd end up with bumps, bruises, and sore places on her body.

NEEDING ANOTHER ANSWER

Mid-July came along and things from the past were still being talked about—some of them quite unpleasant. One day the three of us were talking about all kinds of things from yesteryear and one thing had been nagging me for a very long time—since 1969 to be exact. Because things were going so smoothly, I thought I'd bring the subject up and see if I could get an answer. I was apprehensive but figured "what the heck."

"Mother, can I show you something?"

"What would you like to show me?" she answered.

I leaned close to her and asked if she could see my lower lip. She looked at me sideways so she could see what I was pointing at and focused. "How the hell did you do that?" she asked.

"I didn't do it; you did," I said. "Back in 1969 when you were all bent out of shape because I hadn't gotten all your fish tanks cleaned that day. You hit me with the bottom end of a whiskey decanter."

She went ultra-ballistic on me and said she never did such a thing! Back and forth we went for the next half hour until I wore her down somewhat. I hollered at her to stop denying it because there was no one else in that house at the time that could have done it. I told her that at the time she was so infuriated over those stupid fish tanks that it wouldn't surprise me if she had momentarily blacked out and didn't remember it. I told her how I had spent a ruined weekend at my girlfriend's house and how that next Monday, Mary and I had gone back to the house in Rio Dell and took everything that was still in one piece and loaded it into my car, and how we headed out to leave the county, ended up heading north to Crescent City and on to Grants Pass, Oregon.

She was still furious and ranting and saying she didn't give me that injury. I asked her why in that particular instance she couldn't have either finished cleaning her own fish tanks if it was that critically important to do so or just let me finish them the next day. Then she caught me off guard with her next remark. "What fish tanks?"

"The twenty-two fish tanks you had on that big custom-made bench table in the kitchen of that house," I said.

Mother looked at me like I was out to lunch. I told her she

wasn't going to pull that stunt on me and make like she didn't know what I was talking about. There were over $500 worth of fish in those tanks and they sure as hell weren't mine! She just kept going berserk on me.

"If you can't give me a straight answer to that question, you are a poor excuse for a woman, a mother, and a member of the human race to inflict that kind of damage on your own son."

I'm not proud of my response but I couldn't stop. Everything, the years of pain, just came gushing out of me. I said other things that really stung her, but it was too late. The words were already in the air. She sank down in the recliner and didn't say anything more. Right then and there a picture of Thumper from the Walt Disney movie, "Bambi," popped into my mind. There's a scene when his mother asks him to think about what his father had told him. "Now Thumper, what did your Father teach you?" And Thumper quotes, "If you can't say something nice, don't say nothing at all."

MOVIE WISDOM

The long ago childhood memory of Thumper's answer is interesting. A seed of good character had been planted from a timeless child's movie. A young boy had digested those words. Maybe it's because of a private longing to cling tight to his father's words. Whatever the reason, wisdom grew. Thumper's words brought comfort. In an instant, once Charles had lost his temper and said awful things, he knew the insult cycle had been a lousy way to communicate—and it sure lacked respect. He felt bad.

Don't overlook how fast the Holy Spirit brought Charles

under conviction. This example is clear evidence of a heart that is tender. Good might seem to be buried deep, and we might want to suppress its presence, but despite unfair treatment and years of suffering, compassionate thoughts return to those who love the Lord. The Holy Spirit wastes no time reminding us of a better choice.

Why? Because Jesus tells us in Matthew 12:37 that: "Words are powerful; take them seriously. Words can be your salvation. Words can also be your damnation" (MSG). Careless words will prick our conscience. That's a good thing. A pricked conscience leads to feeling sorrowful, which makes room for anger to give way to a quieter spirit.

ANOTHER HONEST CONVERSATION

Even though we sat and talked for almost three more hours, I never tried to be bossy, accusing, demeaning or condemning again. I did clearly lay out one thing in front of her that opened the conversation again.

"Mom, during the last twenty some odd years I have repeatedly tried building a bridge across a space bigger than the Grand Canyon to try to talk to you. Every time you uncaringly and cruelly snubbed me and blew up my attempt to continue to build that bridge. If you'll look back honestly, you'll see at least two dozen bridges hanging incomplete out over the rim of the canyon."

She sat there looking like she was trying to see what I had so clearly described. She took a deep breath, let it out, and said, "Yeah, I see it."

"Thank you," I replied, feeling we'd made some progress at last. Mother finally admitted she blew up all my attempts to mend

things between us. We talked in generalities for a while, trying to keep from rubbing each other the wrong way again. One thing began to bother me. I was afraid I had made a huge mistake moving her in here, so close to Rachel and me. Time would tell.

Personally I didn't want the war to start up again and destroy the progress we'd made. I guess after going through all that I had to put up with in my life it's understandable to feel leery and untrusting to a certain extent. I feel I will keep expecting the hammer to fall again for a very long time.

Forgiving my mother is something I am not sure I have done yet. Sorry to say, I feel at this moment I'm still too hardened. We both have some serious road-building to do. My mother is going to have to show me she is serious in trying to earn my trust. Then hopefully, our relationship will be repaired and I will be softened and able to tell her that I forgive her and really feel forgiveness on the inside.

STRUGGLING WITH FORGIVENESS

Charles had successfully examined his own words and the conversation resumed in a nonthreatening way. He confronted the past hurts and received validation from his mother. That day some positive progress was made.

Remember that forgiveness is very different from reconciliation. Forgiveness requires only a one-way action. It calls for the wounded individual to give up his anger and desire for revenge against the person who has wronged him, regardless of the behaviors of the other person.

Reconciliation, on the other hand, involves both parties. The perpetrator of the pain chooses to apologize for his or her wrongdoing and asks to be forgiven. The injured party accepts the apology as genuine and the relationship is given a chance at a new beginning.

Ephesians 4:32 instructs us with godly wisdom: "Be kind and compassionate to one another, forgiving each other, just as in Christ God forgave you."

To feel good inside our own skin it's smart to choose to forgive. We'll be blessed with an inner peace the world cannot give. God says so.

FEELINGS OF UNEASINESS

The second week of June, 2010 began with a feeling of uneasiness when we stopped by Mom's place. She kept nervously tapping her hands on the arms of her recliner and saying things that seemed odd or out of place like, "Rachel, you are such a good girl." Rachel is a grown woman and four years older than me!

July 2010 – Mother was dealing with a cold and didn't want to go out to eat. Instead, she told us to go to Taco Bell and get all of us something to eat. We did. The evening was going very nice. We watched some TV and talked. Later, Mother said she was feeling poorly and wanted to go to bed early. Rachel and I thanked her for the dinner and went home.

Over the next couple months, Mother had more falling incidents. Her doctor said it was nothing to worry about. But I wondered about the doctor's lack of concern. The falls happened three or four times a month. She did not use her walker or cane when she moved about in the apartment. Without those helps, she was very shaky and unsteady.

Rachel, Paula (Rachel's daughter), and I started noticing

something else as the weeks passed. Mother had become increasingly depressed and far more verbally abusive to people. She would get mad at the smallest things. If she didn't get her absolute way at all times, there was hell to pay for whoever she decided to vent her rage at. She didn't just get mad—a volcano erupted! Other times she covered her ears to block us out and started yelling NA-NA-NA-NA. The screaming rose up to overpower the talk and her feet started stomping on the floor. The go-to excuse was, "I'm eighty-eight years old and I can act any way I want."

"Why do you want to throw a tantrum like a two-year-old?" I asked.

"I have no social life. I don't care if I wake up in the morning or not. I just sit here every day in this apartment and go nowhere. I sit here every day and watch TV all day."

"Why did you quit going to the senior center? I thought you liked hanging out with those people."

The question made her mad. "None of your business!" was the reply.

I'd struck a raw nerve.

"Mom, did you open your mouth down there and get someone or a bunch of people upset with you? Did they ask you to leave and not come back?"

She blew up like Mt. St. Helens! Her rage told me all I needed to know.

October came around. Mother was in a foul argumentative funk three out of seven days a week. Rachel now only went along with me to visit Mom twice a week because she couldn't stand my mother's constant tirades. One day Rachel told Mother that she didn't like the way she treated me, that her son was busting his butt for her. That only made Mom madder. "I'll do as I damn well please," she said. With that, Rachel left.

And me—I got in Mother's face and came down hard. "You're cruel, spiteful, and vicious! You're hateful, unappreciative, and don't care who you hurt or insult. I'm ashamed, insulted, and offended by your actions. Now pick up that phone. Call Rachel and ask her nicely to come back so you can apologize to her. You may get away with treating me like a dog, but you won't insult my wife. That's where I draw the line."

I was boiling mad. It all rolled out like Noah's flood. I couldn't stop it. Over and over she hollered obscenities about me and my wife as I left the apartment.

No sooner had I walked in my door than the phone rang. Mother still wanted to yell. This time she told me, "Forget about getting the $300 a month for being my caretaker."

"Fine! The money is not worth putting up with the abuse."

I hung up the phone, took Rachel in my arms, and apologized for my mother's conduct.

After ten minutes of holding each other close, we sat down on the couch and I started to cry. I was upset, insulted, and hurting. All of a sudden, a window opened in my mind and everything from five years old to nineteen years old that my mother had said or done to me came flooding back. It was like watching a video replay of everything I had endured all those long years.

I felt so old, so very, very old. Why hadn't I seen the warning signs? She was back to her old Jekyll and Hyde self.

Four days later I went back to Mother's long enough to vacuum the floors and empty the garbage. Later I took the mail to her.

"Oh, it's you," she said.

"Are you all right?" I asked.

She told me she was planning to make a pot of soup for dinner. She told me Ebby missed both me and Rachel. So I paid a lot of attention to Ebby and gave him lots of love and tummy rubs. He purred all over. She then asked about Rachel. We talked for about ten minutes and I told her I had to get going. She gave me a big hug and said she loved me.

I couldn't say anything more than, "Yeah, I know." I left. Forty minutes later I was behind a studio camera taping programs.

THE CYCLE OF ABUSE

Huge shifts between angry outbursts and displays of affection. What is real? Both. What can be trusted? Not a lot. Mother had cooled down her anger, possibly even felt a bit ashamed, and now thought she could mend fences with a pot of soup. Of course, soup won't erase the problems.

The cycle of abuse is just that—a cycle. What goes up must come down and round and round it goes. The abuser's fuse gets lit, she rides that angry crest for a while, but eventually returns to a quieter phase. This lasts until the next cycle of abuse is set in motion.

WARNING SIGNS

Three days later Rachel went to Mother's with me. I'm glad she did. I just don't know what was going on with my mother, but from what Paula, Rachel, and I had been seeing over the last eight months there were warning signs of senility, dementia, or Alzheimer's. Paula had been working as an aide for almost ten years and I had worked as an aide for four years in assisted living. We both knew the signs of mental breakdown.

When I took Mother to the doctor, he couldn't seem to find anything wrong with her. That didn't jive with what we were seeing. I found myself wishing she'd fly into a blind rage in front of the doctor so he'd take this seriously. That didn't happen.

It really upset me that things were going down this way. Just as I was getting my mother back, something like this was happening and taking her further away from me. Life just wasn't fair! And the most distressing thing was that, there wasn't a thing medically that could be done to stop its progression.

On October 30, Rachel and I went over to visit Mother. She showed us a big bruise on the back of her hand that was bluish black and green and a little larger than a silver dollar. When I asked her how she'd done that she told us she'd tripped over her cat and fell to the floor hitting her hand on the wooden bedside stand as she fell. I offered to take her to the doctor, but she didn't think that was necessary.

The next day, October 31st, I went to Mom's without Rachel. In hindsight, I wish Rachel had come along.

"Hi Mom. What's going on?" I asked.

"Nothing. Watching TV. Watching that fat [obscenities] Oprah Winfrey."

"If you hate her, why do you persist in watching her? You have more than 250 other channels you could be watching. And why do you keep degrading and bad-mouthing people all the time?"

I defended Oprah's reputation right there. "Oprah would not be on ABC, or be opening up her own network, or be so popular if what you are saying was remotely true."

My mother started yelling. "My sister lives in Chicago. She told me and she ought to know about Oprah!"

Right there I knew she'd stepped off the end of the pier.

"Mom, right after moving in here, you told Rachel and me that your sister lived in Ft. Wayne, Indiana, and that she had died about ten years ago."

Mother came totally unglued. She yelled and stomped her feet on the floor. "No I didn't! No I didn't! No I didn't!"

Over and over the phrase was repeated like a broken record. She began to pound her fists on the arms of her recliner and was raving furious. At no time was I trying to start an argument. My intent was to remind her of a previous conversation.

It was on that day that I told my mother she was telling lies and that if she kept on living and acting in such an angry ways I might be forced to put her back into an assisted living facility for her own good. At that, she went out of her mind and screamed all the more. I tried to calm her down. To no avail.

All of a sudden she jumped up. "Get out! Get out! Get out! I'm calling the police!"

"You've just gone overboard and are indeed stark raving crazy as a loon!" I said. "You do need to be put in the nut house." Yes, I know that was a very poor choice of words, but that's what popped out of my mouth.

She grabbed the phone. I grabbed for it and got a thumb and forefinger hold. Ninety-nine percent of the phone was in both of her hands. She wrenched sideways and I lost my grip on the handset. In the jerking of the handset, the other end of the cord came out of the base. She started swinging that handset over her head. I thought she was going to hit me and ducked one blow.

"You are a raving maniac!" I hollered. "I am leaving and never, ever, coming back! I don't care if you fall over with a heart attack. I won't come back ever again!"

With that I was out the door and went straight home to fill Rachel in on what had just happened. She just shook her head and said it sounded like my mother had finally lost it. That was how October 31st ended.

UNREALISTIC EXPECTATIONS

A whole lot of things went wrong during this conversation. If indeed dementia was part of his mother's health status, there would naturally be big gaps in memory. Long-term memory would be easier to recall than a short-term memory of only a few months or days.

My maternal grandmother had dementia and couldn't understand why her mother didn't come to see her. The answer was simple. Her mother had passed away years earlier. In fact, I never met my great-grandmother. The memories Grandma had held onto the best were those made decades earlier. Her mind centered on the good times with her mama. Every visit would start out the same. I would gently reacquaint her with family relationships. Soon she'd reenter what was happening in the present and our talk would pick up and go from there.

Charles had not realized that his expectations for her behaviors were unrealistic. His mother did not see life as he did. She had prejudices and, according to his observations, a measure of mental impairment. We cannot demand that others change. What we can and should do is work to improve ourselves by figuring out how to cope with difficult people in less frustrating ways. Whether they change or not is not meant to become our responsibility even if we get dirtied by their behaviors.

In hindsight, the worst thing he did that day was to threaten his mother with the possibility of going back to an assisted living center or, worse yet, to the nut house. This was not the right way to get his message across. Threats cause others to get defensive—not cooperative.

BIG TROUBLE WAS BREWING

Until midafternoon, November 1, 2010 was a good day. There was no indication more trouble was brewing. At three o'clock Rachel and I walked across the parking lot to Food 4 Less. A police car rolled past us and parked in front of another apartment. We paid no attention and continued on our way to buy groceries. Ten minutes later we were in the dairy section and saw two cops wandering around in the store. As we were getting eggs, the next thing I knew, a set of hands roughly gripped both of my shoulders! They pinned me in place. I asked them just what the hell they thought they were doing. What was going on?

I was told I was under arrest. Under arrest! For what? By now at least half the customers in the store were gathered around to see what was going on. They ordered me to put my hands behind my back like some kind of rude storm troopers! This was turning into a nightmare in the middle of the day. What had I done? I hadn't broken any laws. I was getting mad.

One officer told me to shut up and quit arguing. I demanded my rights to be told what I was being arrested for. The law clearly states that they were to tell me. The bigger cop told me they didn't have to tell me nothing. I demanded to see the warrant. They said that's not how their law worked. Can you believe that? They told me to shut up or they'd include disorderly conduct on top of everything else.

Rachel was standing frozen in place. She didn't know what was going on either. I tried to hand my wallet to her but one of the cops grabbed it out of her hand and started rifling through it without permission or a warrant. I tried to hand her my keys so she could get back in the apartment since she'd left her keys at home. The cops went through my wallet and found my driver's license and took it out and put my license in their shirt pocket. They never allowed me to give my keys to Rachel. The bully cops didn't care about something like that. A lot of illegal search and seizure took place that afternoon.

The cops waltzed me out the front door of the store and took me all the way back across the parking lot to our apartment parking lot where they finally took my keys and put them in the front door so Rachel would find them. Would you believe they wouldn't let her come along as we walked across the parking lot? They told her to stay in the store. How rude, crude, and crass. Once at the patrol car, the one cop finally told me what I was being arrested for. I was under arrest for . . . "Domestic violence!"

I started laughing. "Who had I supposedly committed this outrageous act against?"

"Do you know a Josephine ____?"

At that moment you could have knocked me clear across town with a pigeon feather. When I snapped back to the moment, I asked him if he was joking.

"No. I am not joking."

Again he asked me if I knew the name. I said, "Yes."

I told him Josephine was my mentally off-balance, delirious, and dementia-affected mother. He said she didn't seem to be afflicted mentally because she had sworn out a warrant against me.

My head was whirling! Nonetheless, I was stuffed into the patrol car and taken to jail.

Five and a half hours later I was allowed to make my one phone call. Of course, I called Rachel and filled her in on what was happening. She exploded when I told her what the charge was and who put the charge on me. I told her to get a notepad and gave her some instructions of who to call and what to do next to get me out of jail. I asked her to read it back to me to make sure she had it right. Rachel was really rattled, mad, and crying all at the same time. She was on-fire furious that my dear sweet mother, the woman we'd helped so much, would have the nerve to do something like this!

HEART TROUBLES

The holding cell had air blowing into it that was so cold you could hang sides of beef in there. I was stressed out to the max over this whole ridiculous fiasco. Later that evening, I started having chest pains. I do have a confirmed arrhythmia of the heart, so I called for a guard. Twenty minutes later one came down the hallway. I hollered that I needed a doctor and was taken to what seemed like the other end of the building where a doctor ran an EKG. My heart was reading kind of crazy. My blood pressure was taken and nitro given to me. Three hours later, after EKGs every twenty minutes, the doctor was satisfied that the incident had passed. I was taken to another cell and monitored until morning when I was taken to a regular cell.

OUT ON BAIL

Later that day I appeared before the judge via a video link. My bail was lowered to $500. As soon as possible, I got Rachel on the phone, filled her in on what had happened since my arrest, and she set about arranging bail. Three hours later I walked out the door and headed home.

Neither one of us slept well that night. Tossing and turning was how the hours were spent. The only condition put on me by the judge was a "No Contact" order. That meant I couldn't be anywhere near my mother. This, too, seemed ridiculous since we lived only 200 feet apart! To even stick my nose outside the door I had to first make sure she was nowhere in sight. In many ways it felt like I was being held prisoner in my own home. I was given a public defender and told my status hearing was set for February 12th at 8 a.m.

Rachel and I went about some of our own investigative work, beginning with the assisted living center where Mother had been evicted. We had a nice long talk with the new administrator. After explaining what had happened, she agreed to bring the files on my mother to both my attorney's office and into court along with a couple of the aides who had worked directly with my mother. Unfortunately, a few days later we were told by the attorney that the District Attorney's office would contest the papers because they were not from a licensed doctor or psychiatrist and originated from an assisted living center. Our big ace in the hole got trumped. We were back at square one.

Luck made an appearance a couple days later when we found out that two days prior to the big blowup with Mother, and my arrest, Mother had been out talking to some of her neighbors who were also friends of ours. It seems that on October 29, 2010, she was showing them the big bruise on her hand. When they asked her how she got the bruise, she told all three of them that she had stumbled over her cat and had fallen to the floor and hit her hand on the bedside stand. Glory hallelujah! Just the evidence I needed. Once again the attorney was happy and spoke with each one of those neighbors.

The next lightning bolt to hit came from the District Attorney's office. He said he would very easily get the three witnesses' testimony dismissed from the proceedings on the grounds that these people had known me for so long and there was a strong possibility that they could lie. I was not happy about this turn of events at all. In my mind, this court wouldn't bat an eye finding Jesus guilty, too.

I told my attorney I was not real happy with this crooked and illegal turn of events and that I was not happy with her either. I told her I fully expected her to go into court and get this whole stupid mess thrown out of court and then turn around and go after my mother like a starving alligator and nail her for filing a false report to police.

SCARED SPITLESS

Two days later the attorney called and told me the only thing she could get the D.A. to agree to was if I pleaded, "No Contest." If I did that, then the D.A. would let the case drop with my night in jail to be credited as time served and then one-year summary probation, which technically was no probation at all.

"What! That's not what I expected you to do," I said, in no uncertain terms.

"I know," she said. "But hear me out. The prosecutor on this case is a woman, a woman who is a bulldog with a bad reputation for sending people way down the river on domestic violence charges."

That scared me spitless right there! If I went to jail for more than twenty days, I would lose my Social Security, and I absolutely could not afford to have that happen. My check each month paid our rent and utilities. Without that check, there would be no roof over our heads. So I told my attorney, "Damn the torpedoes and full speed ahead. Go for the offer."

WALKING FREE

Thirty minutes later I walked out of that courtroom technically a free man. Rachel and I celebrated over Chinese food for lunch. We had miraculously survived my mother's dirty little game.

February 14, 2011, and everything was over. It did not go the way I had wanted it to go, but in the end I did win and in another way, I lost. I kept my freedom and didn't go to jail. I didn't lose my Social Security and I was free to go anywhere I wanted at any time and was not accountable to the courts. The way I lost was with court costs, attorney fees, and the loss of my bail money.

A week later, Rachel and I were sitting out on our patio when a U-Haul truck pulled up in front of Mother's door. A couple guys got out and walked up to her door. The next thing we saw was the truck being loaded with Mother's belongings. Two hours later they pulled out onto the street.

Good riddance! At last I could breathe easier. The wicked witch of the west was gone. A couple days later the final papers *including the "No Contact" order arrived in an envelope. I am to have absolutely no knowledge of my mother's whereabouts. The irony of the whole thing is that her new address was printed right on the front page. Rachel and I laughed for fifteen minutes— laughed until we cried.*

If you are ready...

Reach for Fresh Joy *[for the abused]*

> "Blessed are those who find wisdom,
> those who gain understanding,
> for she is more profitable than silver
> and yields better returns than gold."
> Proverbs 3:13–14

What message had the "Bambi" movie taught Charles?
_____
_____

Have you ever applied Thumper's wisdom?_____
When?
_____
_____
_____

How did that help your circumstances?
___
___

Describe the difference between forgiving someone and reconciling with someone who has wronged you:
___
___
___

Charles was wronged again. This one was a whopper! What was his initial reaction?
___
___
___

Has your abuser given you hope and then wronged you again?
___

What happened?
___
___
___

What unavoidable consequences did you suffer because of your offender's actions?
___
___
___

The Bible has something to say about seeking revenge: "Do not take revenge, my dear friends, but leave room for God's wrath, for it is written: 'It is mine to avenge; I will repay'." (Romans 12:19).

Write a prayer asking the Lord to take all feelings of revenge from you:

_____
_____
_____
_____
_____
_____
_____

If you are ready...

Reach for Fresh Hope *[for the abuser]*

"But the fruit of the Spirit is love, joy, peace,
forbearance [patience], kindness, goodness,
faithfulness, gentleness and self-control.
Against such things there is no law."
Galatians 5:22–23

If you are a Christian, there should be evidence of Christ-like fruit—the fruit of the Spirit—growing in your life. How is your fruit maturing? ____ good ____ not at all ____ excellent

Which fruit qualities are the easiest for you to grow?
_____

Which of the nine qualities are the hardest for you to grow?
_____

Describe how the absence of good fruit has harmed your children/family?
_____
_____
_____
_____
_____
_____

"Do not be deceived: God cannot be mocked. A man reaps what he sows.

> Whoever sows to please their flesh, from the
> flesh will reap destruction; whoever sows to please the Spirit,
> from the Spirit will reap eternal life."
> Galatians 6:7–8

Be hopeful. You can cultivate the fruit of the Spirit in your life. Begin to envision a bumper crop of love, joy, peace, patience, kindness, goodness, faithfulness, gentleness and self-control growing inside of you. God will help you to plant and plow, feed and weed.

Write one doable action step beside each individual fruit quality. Keep this exercise simple and achievable.

Love: _____

Joy: _____

Peace: _____

Patience:_____

Kindness: _____

Goodness: _____

Faithfulness: _____

Gentleness:_____

Self-control: _____

> "Let us not become weary in doing good,
> for at the proper time we will reap a
> harvest if we do not give up."
> Galatians 6:9

Forgiveness is letting go. It is the relaxation of your "death grip" on the pain you feel.

Forgiveness is not a feeling first. It is a choice that goes beyond feelings; it is an activity of the will. You may respond, "If I were to forgive someone when I didn't feel like it, I would be a hypocrite." This is another great lie. If you forgive even when you don't feel like it, you are a responsible person—not a hypocrite.[14]

— Tim LaHaye and Bob Phillips

THIRTEEN
Letting Go

Just when we thought all of the trouble was over, another blow came from a totally unexpected direction. A thirty-day eviction notice arrived from our rental agency. I was already reeling from all the grief my mother had caused in my life, and now the hope I'd felt the last two years had been sunk when this bombshell dropped. The old line, "If it weren't for bad luck, I'd have no luck at all," seemed to describe my life.

After all Rachel and I had gone through, I was tired of being pushed around, buffaloed, intimidated, ripped off, and lied about. Without any discussion, after eleven years of being a model tenant, I was being tossed out like a piece of trash. Talking to the rental agency did no good despite arguing until I was blue in the face.

We searched and searched for three weeks for a place to rent and were turned down nine times. In desperation, I put an ad in our local buy-and-sell paper that panned out. We found a place on the west side of town, talked with the landlord, and were approved. Four days later Rachel and I moved in to a considerably smaller apartment that cost $25 more per month. After some downsizing and getting a storage shed, life felt like it was settling down.

I am looking into ways to sue my ex-mother for all our hardship, inconvenience, worry, stress, and expense and anything else I can nail her for. After what she pulled on me, she needs to have someone pull some kind of legal action that will hit her right between the eyes and knock her off her feet.

I hate to sound this vengeful against my own mother, but after all that has transpired, all I've endured at her hands since I was a small boy, all those years of physical hurt, emotional scars, financial loss, and three wives who up and left because of her filthy insults, it's hard to think otherwise.

The physical scars I will carry to my grave are nearly impossible to forgive. Maybe God will help me with that. I am aware of the old adage, "To forgive is divine," or "To forgive is the Christian thing to do," but I'm finding that step really hard to take. I'm just one little insignificant person with all the human faults that people have. So I guess I may be damned to hell when I die for feeling the way I do. I don't know. Only Jesus and God will make that decision when the time comes. They alone are perfect, all knowledgeable, and full of so much more compassion than I could ever have.

FORGIVENESS EXPLAINED

Are you also troubled about forgiveness? Do you feel forgiven? The simplest demonstration of God's grace and forgiveness toward all of us is found in John 3:16–17:

> For God so loved the world that he gave his one and only Son, that whoever believes in him shall not perish but have eternal life. For God did not send his Son into the world to condemn the world, but to save the world through him.

The biggest takeaway message of the Bible is that we are all significant and greatly loved! To feel like our lives don't matter is a terrible lie. In the eyes of God, we are precious. He's made salvation uncomplicated. The *only* thing we have to do to be forgiven is to say "Yes" to Jesus. After that, the matter is settled and our names are written in the Book of Life. Heaven awaits all who believe.

Being acceptable to God is not based on our own merit but on the righteousness of Jesus Christ. Not one of us—not even Pope Francis himself—can ever wash ourselves clean enough to be in *right* standing with Almighty God. Our forgiveness of sin and salvation is not based on human effort but rests solely on the atoning blood of Jesus Christ. Upon accepting Jesus as Savior, God sees us through His Son, without spot, perfect before the throne, and dressed in the whitest of white robes. All sin, past, present, or future, is pardoned. That's the simplistic beauty of God's amazing grace.

The bigger problem with forgiveness is us. A whole lot of people don't want to let their offender off the hook for the injustice that's been done. But letting go through the portal of forgiveness is what is needed to free ourselves from yesterday's painful memories. Dr. Tim Clinton's explanation reveals the personal benefits to be gained.

> All relationships demand the deep oil of forgiveness. When we forgive it breaks the poisonous cycle of revenge, and allows the broken to walk in peace. The Jesus way is always the way of forgiveness. We forgive to free ourselves and to get our lives back. His way is the way that gives the future hope . . . a hope that can turn your life around.[15]

Because God has forgiven us so much, forgiving others becomes easier. At first this might not be something we want to do, but it is the righteous thing to do. Forgiveness is the greatest love story ever told and the heart of the Gospel message. God loves every one of us enough to set us free from our sins. In turn, He instructs His kids to pardon those who have treated them badly.

Most of us have recited The Lord's Prayer. That prayer, found in Matthew 6:12, affirms what we are to do: *"Forgive us our debts, as we also have forgiven our debtors."* Those who hunger to be set free will apply this step. The choice is ours to make. But as long as the focus is on revenge, the joy of the Lord will not be felt.

Rest assured that God will take care of the evildoers in His way and His timing. No one escapes God's watchful eye. Isn't it time to let the bitterness go? Isn't it time to be free of those who have committed wrongs against you?

I pray God's best path will be chosen. When revenge is left to Him, the hardened heart finds its peace. Our tomorrows are freed up. Understand that Jesus also wore a crown of thorns, despite the deep wounds He endured. He could have taken every bad guy out—but he didn't. Instead, He chose the cross. Jesus let love triumph. His example shows us how to hate sin but not the sinner. Forgiveness is the cure for wounded emotions. Forgiveness is the greatest act of love one human being can give to another.

TODAY I'VE LET GO

Our landlord is a really cool guy. We hardly ever see him, and when he does show up, he's always happy, upbeat, and very easygoing. We have a great big beautiful park across the street where Rachel and I can walk the path around the park every day or just go over and sit on a bench in the sun and soak up some rays and watch the day go by. It's nice and relaxing. If I'm real ambitious, I can fly my kites and really be one with nature. In the evenings and on mild nights we can sit and listen to the frogs croaking in the wetland area of the park. What a simple, totally pleasant, experience.

Sometimes we can walk down the sidewalk almost two miles, stop in at stores, window-shop, or go in and browse or shop for real. Our patio is a great place to sit and look across the street while drinking sweet sun tea that was brewed on top of the breaker panels on the side of our apartment. Life is being enjoyed.

Our frayed and shattered nerves are slowly mending. Rachel and I are starting to smile again. We're beginning to feel that life is good again. We've started to pull ourselves out of the financial disaster my mother had set in motion.

And, my mother's life has a twist of irony. She's back in foster care in the town she told us for two years she absolutely hated and despised. All I have asked of the facility is to be notified when she passes. I'm not sure why that matters to me, but it seems important to attend the service.

I guess there is some kind of retribution after all. All of this has made me feel so much better, realizing that all of my life I've just been a wandering orphan. I have never had a mother's steady love. At last I am content with that truth and happy with what I do have. I am blessed with a wife that I love without reservation, a very spoiled calico cat named Meg, and 210,000 records in my collection. Life is good.

I close now wishing everyone peace and long life. May God give you happiness and contentment all of your days.

MOVING ON

Letting go feels good. The fight is over. The body relaxes. Breathing returns to a normal rhythm.

Despite being denied access to see his mother, which is for the best, Charles contacted the care facility and asked to be notified when she passes away. He wants to attend the service. The relationship still needs some closure, but his heart is not hard. That in itself is beautiful.

The good news today is that Charles Rice has let go. The future looks bright. He's decided to move forward with his life and leave the things he cannot change in God's hands. And so can you.

It seems fitting to include a quote from one of America's greatest military leaders. General George S. Patton once said, "The test of success is not what you do when you are on top. Success is how high you bounce when you hit bottom."

If you are ready...

Reach for Fresh Joy *[for the abused]*

"Forget the former things; do not dwell on the past.
See, I am doing a new thing! Now it springs up;
do you not perceive it? I am making a way in the wilderness
and streams in the wasteland."
Isaiah 43:18–19

Count your blessings: _____

_____

Forgiveness is part of letting go of our hurts. Who do you need to forgive? _____

How would you describe forgiveness?
_____
_____
_____

What "new" thing might God be wanting you to do?
_____
_____
_____

Are you at a point where you want to let go of the past?
_____
_____

What steps will you take?
_____
_____
_____

Is there someone who will encourage you to move forward?
_____

Who? _____

    Give thanks to the Lord. You are a survivor. God's promises have your name on them. The future is bright.

> Satan wants us to have a negative attitude
> and to feel hopeless, but God's Word says we should be
> "prisoners of hope."... Don't let your past failures
> leave you hopeless about your future success. Your future
> has no room in it for the failures of the past.[16]
> — Joyce Meyer

If you are ready...

Reach for Fresh Hope *[for the abuser]*

> "As obedient children, do not conform to the
> evil desires you had when you lived in ignorance."
> 1 Peter 1:14

The choice is yours. You are free to do as you want. Will you live your life in a way that pleases the Lord, and be blessed, or give in to abusive behaviors and suffer the consequences? This book has given you plenty of reasons why it's best to live life God's way. Let's present four future scenarios.

1. What would your family be like in two years if the abuse stopped?

_____
_____
_____
_____
_____

2. What will your family be like in two years if you continue to lose your temper and abuse your children?

_____
_____
_____
_____
_____

3. When your children leave home, what do you want them to remember about you?

_____
_____
_____
_____
_____

4. Do you want your children to grow up to be just like you?
_____

Why or why not?
_____
_____
_____
_____

> "By wisdom a house is built,
> and through understanding it is established;
> through knowledge its rooms
> are filled with rare and beautiful treasures."
> Proverbs 24:3–4

One More Thing

Charles asked that a copy of the "Written Statement" given by his three neighbors, and presented by his public defender to the District Attorney, be included in this book. To maintain privacy, names are omitted.

I, _____, (Witness name) do hereby swear and attest that on November 1, 2010, Charles Rice was falsely accused of Domestic Violence by his mentally unstable mother, Josephine _____, (pronounced ____). Charles Rice was illegally arrested, jailed, tried and convicted. Mrs. _____ received the injuries and resultant bruises on her hands as a result of tripping over her cat and falling to the floor, hitting both hands on her wooden bedside stand as she fell. She showed me the bruises two days before her claim against Charles Rice. Mrs. ____ freely and openly admitted this to me in the parking lot of our apartment units.

_____ (Signature)
Print name, address, and phone number

A Mother's love lives on... she remembers [her child's] merry laugh, the joyful shout of his childhood, the opening promise of his youth.

— Washington Irving

Washington Irving was an American author of the early 19th century best known for his books, *The Legend of Sleepy Hollow* and *Rip Van Winkle*.

THE GOAL:
GOD'S DESIGN FOR A WOMAN

If possible, set aside that truckload of personal mommy hurts long enough to become acquainted with God's blueprint for a woman. In a perfect world, she's good—never furious or scary. A godly mother possesses noble character. She cares deeply for her family and responds in love, even when tough love is needed. And when God's intended design doesn't take shape in a woman's life, good mothering skills are missing and precious children suffer. The way to describe godly womanhood is to read what the Bible has to say in Proverbs 31:10–31:

> [10] A wife of noble character who can find? She is worth far more than rubies.
>
> [11] Her husband has full confidence in her and lacks nothing of value.
>
> [12] She brings him good, not harm, all the days of her life.
>
> [13] She selects wool and flax and works with eager hands.

¹⁴ She is like the merchant ships, bringing her food from afar.

¹⁵ She gets up while it is still night; she provides food for her family and portions for her female servants.

¹⁶ She considers a field and buys it; out of her earnings she plants a vineyard.

¹⁷ She sets about her work vigorously; her arms are strong for her tasks.

¹⁸ She sees that her trading is profitable, and her lamp does not go out at night.

¹⁹ In her hand she holds the distaff and grasps the spindle with her fingers.

²⁰ She opens her arms to the poor and extends her hands to the needy.

²¹ When it snows, she has no fear for her household; for all of them are clothed in scarlet.

²² She makes coverings for her bed; she is clothed in fine linen and purple.

²³ Her husband is respected at the city gate, where he takes his seat among the elders of the land.

²⁴ She makes linen garments and sells them, and supplies the merchants with sashes.

> [25] She is clothed with strength and dignity; she can laugh at the days to come.
>
> [26] She speaks with wisdom, and faithful instruction is on her tongue.
>
> [27] She watches over the affairs of her household and does not eat the bread of idleness.
>
> [28] Her children arise and call her blessed; her husband also, and he praises her:
>
> [29] "Many women do noble things, but you surpass them all."
>
> [30] Charm is deceptive, and beauty is fleeting; but a woman who fears the LORD is to be praised.
>
> [31] Honor her for all that her hands have done, and let her works bring her praise at the city gate.

Granted, this picture is high and lofty for any woman to live up to—not just mothers. While our humanity keeps us from achieving perfection, it does not stop us from striving to reach this standard. With God's help, women really do come close to the mark. Children really do arise and speak blessings about their mothers.

When an authentic God-centered woman begins to emerge, those she loves are blessed. Two of our nation's most beloved Presidents spoke well of their mothers. George Washington said, "My mother was the most beautiful woman I ever saw. All

I am I owe to my mother. I attribute all my success in life to the moral, intellectual and physical education I received from her." And Abraham Lincoln voiced, "All that I am or ever hope to be, I owe to my angel mother." What beautiful tributes! Washington and Lincoln became men of strong character and great leaders. Both gave credit to the positive influence of their mothers.

Unfortunately, not all children can praise their mother. Unless a mother picks up her role as God defines it, her ability to become a woman of noble character will be hard to achieve. Nevertheless, one thing is certain. Every mother influences her child's development, good or bad, from the moment that baby is born. She is the number one teacher of early life lessons. From her knee, a child's character begins to take shape. She shows what it means to give and receive love. Mothers are typically wired with protective instincts that impart feelings of safety and warnings of danger. And yet, some children are so poorly mothered that their earliest lessons center around fear, tears, pain, and the necessity to survive abuse.

Please don't throw this book across the room. Victims of child abuse were/are terribly mistreated. Your pain is not being trivialized. But don't persist in thinking all women are bad, unloving, or mean. That's a terrible lie cunningly crafted by the enemy of your soul—Satan. Charles Rice recognized his girlfriend's mother was a good mom, a kind woman, who showed him what a caring mother would act like. She was not at all like his mother.

And ladies, please don't believe that because you were abused as a child, or because you now abuse your own child, that there is no hope of being a godly woman. That's another one of Satan's vile lies. Change is possible. God loves you! As long as life endures, with God's help, anyone can move past the past. Every wrongful behavior can be replaced by one that accomplishes good from this day forward. Reach out for help. Pray. God is near.

Walk away from denial and the lies you've adopted as truth. Admit those faults. Choose to believe God is who He says He is. That He is the Creator of all mankind, that He created you in His image, and that He loves you with an unfailing love that endures forever. Once these basic truths are absorbed, the perception of self will transform into a sincere belief that you are a person whose worth far exceeds the rarest of rubies.

> Psalm 139:13–14: For you created my inmost being; you knit me together in my mother's womb. I praise you because I am fearfully and wonderfully made; your works are wonderful, I know that full well.

> Psalm 108:4: For great is your love, higher than the heavens; your faithfulness reaches to the skies.

> Psalm 145:18: The LORD is near to all who call on him, to all who call on him in truth.

Endnotes

Beth Moore, *Stepping Up: A Journey Through the Psalms of Ascent*, p. 112

[2] Gary Jackson Oliver and H. Norman Wright, *When Anger Hits Home*, 1992, Moody Press, p. 39

[3] Kathy Collard Miller, *When Counting to Ten Isn't Enough*, 2003, Xulon Press, p. 14

[4] Brennan Manning, *The Ragamuffin Gospel*, 2000, Multnomah Publishers, p. 158–159

[5] Dr. Tim Clinton and Dr. Gary Sibcy, *Why You Do The Things You Do*, 2006, Thomas Nelson, p. 33

[6] Ron Mehl, *Love Found a Way*, 1999, Waterbrook Press, p. 78

[7] *Psychology Today*, Nov–Dec 2013, Judith Sills, Ph.D., "The Power of No!" p. 58

[8] Pia Mellody with Andrea Wells Miller and J. Keith Miller, *Facing Codependence*, 1989, Harper & Row Publishers, San Francisco, p. 118–119

[9] Beverly Engel, *Healing your Emotional Self*, 2006, John Wiley & Sons, Inc., p.12

[10] Dr. Tim Clinton and Dr. Gary Sibcy, *Why You Do The Things You Do*, 2006, Thomas Nelson, p. 228

[11] John Bradshaw, *Healing the Shame That Binds You*, 1988, Health Communications, Inc., Deerfield Beach, FL, p. 14

[12] Dr. Phil McGraw, *Family First*, 2004, Free Press, p. 129

[13] Dr. Susan Forward, *Toxic Parents*, 1989, Bantam Books, p. 238

[14] Tim LaHaye and Bob Phillips, *Anger Is A Choice*, 1982, Zondervan Publishing, p. 112, 114

[15] Dr. Tim Clinton, "The Oil of Forgiveness," http://www.aacc.net/2014/02/18/the-deep-oil-of-forgiveness-4/

[16] Joyce Meyer, *Approval Addiction*, 2005, Warner Faith, p. 55

NATIONAL STATISTICS ON CHILD ABUSE

Nearly five children die every day in America from abuse and neglect.[1]

In 2011, an estimated 1,570 children died from abuse and neglect in the United States.[2]

In the same year, Children's Advocacy Centers around the country served more than 279,000 child victims of abuse, providing victim advocacy and support to these children and their families. In 2012, this number was nearly 287,000.[3]

2011 NATIONAL ABUSE STATISTICS[2]

- Approximately 681,000 children were victims of maltreatment.

- 46 states reported approximately 3.3 million children received preventive services from Child Protective Services agencies in the United States.

- Children younger than one year had the highest rate of victimization of 21.2 per 1,000 children in the national population of the same age.

- Of the children who experienced maltreatment or abuse, over 75% suffered neglect; more than 15% suffered physical abuse; and just under 10% suffered sexual abuse.

- More than 78% of reported child fatalities as a result of abuse and neglect were caused by one or more of the child victim's parents.

2012 CHILDREN'S ADVOCACY CENTER STATISTICS [3]

Among the nearly 287,000 children served by Children's Advocacy Centers around the country in 2012, the startling statistics include:

- 109,619 children were ages 0 to 6 years
- 103,636 children were ages 7 to 12 years
- 71,840 children were ages 13 to 18 years
- 197,902 children reported sexual abuse
- 49,155 children reported physical abuse
- 196,732 children participated in on-site forensic interviewing at a Children's Advocacy Center

Among the more than 262,000 alleged offenders investigated for instances of child abuse in 2012, the upsetting statistics reveal:

- 147,005 were 18+ years old
- 25,756 were ages 13 to 17 years

- 18,227 were under age 13 years
- 85,699 were a parent or step-parent of the victim
- 125,129 were related or known to the child victim in another way
- 22,055 were an unrelated person the victim knew

---

[1] *Every Child Matters Education Fund (2009). We Can Do Better: Child Abuse and Neglect Deaths in the U.S.* http://www.everychildmatters.org/storage/documents/pdf/reports/wcdbv2.pdf

[2] *U.S. Department of Health and Human Services: Administration for Children & Families. Child Maltreatment 2011.* http://www.acf.hhs.gov/sites/default/files/cb/cm11.pdf

[3] *National Children's Alliance 2012 and 2011 national statistics collected from Children's Advocacy Center members.*

ADDENDUM

Resources

Military families can turn to *www.militaryonesource.mil* The Department of Defense (DoD) is committed to addressing and ending domestic abuse. The Family Advocacy Program (FAP) works to prevent abuse by offering programs to put a stop to domestic abuse before it starts. When abuse does occur, the FAP works to ensure the safety of victims and helps military families overcome the effects of violence and change destructive behavior patterns. FAP staff members are trained to respond to incidents of abuse and neglect, support victims, and offer prevention and treatment. Child abuse and neglect are defined as injury, maltreatment, or neglect to a child that harms or threatens the child's welfare. The FAP will get involved when one of the parties is a military member or, in some cases, a DoD civilian serving at an overseas installation. See *http://www.militaryonesource.mil/phases-military-leadership?content_id=266712*

Child Welfare League of America (CWLA) is a powerful coalition of hundreds of private and public agencies serving vulnerable children and families since 1920. Their expertise, leadership and innovation on policies, programs, and practices helps improve the lives of millions of children in all fifty states. Their impact is felt worldwide. CWLA lists three ways you can help if you suspect a child is suffering from maltreatment:

1. IF IT IS AN EMERGENCY, CALL YOUR LOCAL POLICE DEPARTMENT. They can ensure the immediate safety of a child and get medical attention if needed.

2. Call your state or local child abuse hotline.

3. If you are unsure how to report, contact Childhelp USA® National Child Abuse Hotline by telephone at 1-800-4-A-CHILD® or through their website, *www.childhelpusa.org*, for information about how to report in your community. See *http://www.cwla.org/whowhat/whowhat.htm*

CASA (Court Appointed Special Advocates): This is a national network of community-based trained advocates who are ready to intervene in the courts on behalf of children who are wards of the court. CASAs work in 933 locations throughout the nation. *www.casaforchildren.org*.

Recommended Reading

***Mean Mothers: Overcoming the Legacy of Hurt*,** Peg Streep, Harper Collins Publishers, 2009

This look into the darker side of maternal behavior is accompanied by scientific research, psychology, and experiential relationships between mothers and adult daughters. This book could be considered a resource for both sons and daughters. Truths cross gender lines.

***When Anger Hits Home*,** Gary Jackson Oliver and H. Norman Wright, Moody Press, 1992

Anger is often misused and misunderstood. This book digs deep into anger in a family tree, angry parents, angry children, and tells the truth about when anger crosses the line.

***Battlefield of the Mind*,** Joyce Meyer, Warner Faith, 1995

Tearing down strongholds begins with the mind. Joyce Meyer reveals how to recognize and overcome damaging thought patterns and keep them from influencing the rest of your life.

Approval Addiction, Joyce Meyer, Warner Faith, 2005

Discover how to love yourself and stop struggling for approval.

Family First, Dr. Phil McGraw, Free Press, 2004

Real talk about parenting that doesn't sabotage your own family. Dr. Phil tells what you need to stop doing and what you need to start doing to parent without scarring your children.

Toxic Parents, Dr. Susan Forward with Craig Buck, Bantam Books, 1989

Psychologist Dr. Susan Forward sorts out the legacy of emotional and physical pain caused by toxic parents. Blameless children were betrayed. This book brings truth to those childhood hurts of feeling worthless, unlovable, and inadequate and tells how not to carry them into adulthood.

When Counting to Ten Isn't Enough, Kathy Collard Miller, Xulon Press, 2003

Honest and practical talk to the abuser written by a woman who identifies with that pain. Did you know anger begins with low self-esteem? And that child abuse causes low self-image? This book will help the reader examine and defuse anger. Parental frustration need not be taken out on children.

The Ragamuffin Gospel, Brennan Manning, Multnomah Publishers, 2000

This book presents the beauty of the Gospel message. It is written for the bedraggled, beat-up, and burnt-out. It is for the bent and bruised who feel their lives are a grave disappointment to God, and for smart people who know they are stupid and honest disciples who admit they are scalawags.

Healing for Damaged Emotions, David A. Seamands, Chariot Victor Books, 1991

True to its title, this book is a realistic approach to how to recover from the memories that cause our pain. Unpredictable parents have caused damaged emotions that need healing.

Total Forgiveness, R.T. Kendall, Hodder & Stoughton, 2007

Forgiveness isn't always easy, but it is a gift we can give. As we release those who have hurt us, we receive freedom and blessings. This book explains why forgiveness opens the door to inner peace.

ACKNOWLEDGEMENTS

I am so thankful for my cheerleaders; those special people who gave graciously of their time, talents, energy and expertise throughout this writing journey. The words from Charles Rice were often difficult to write—and yet too compelling not to bring forth. Many mocha moments were spent with my amazing critique partners Tom Fuller, Pamala J. Vincent (www.pamalajvincent.com), and Lindy Batdorf. Thank you for your friendship and eagerness to read this manuscript. Your honest, constructive comments helped me keep a very difficult subject real. In the end, I have been blessed beyond measure.

I owe heartfelt appreciation to my loyal friend, blog talk radio co-host, and multi-published author, Jeannie St. John Taylor (jeanniestjohntaylor.com). Your practical helps and encouragement were perfectly timed. Thank you for believing in this book. You are a priceless gift.

To the unknown voices, those who heard about this book prior to its printing and without hesitation came forth to tell me of your own experience with an angry mother, I applaud you. You reinforced the need to bring out in the open what's been hidden far too long. Furious mothers are the lot of too many vulnerable children.

Those at Ellechor Media, I appreciate you so much. I express thanks to Rochelle Carter, Sharon Jenkins, and D.E. West. Your hard work has birthed a book of excellent quality. Your passion to help the abused resonates with my heart. God bless you.

About the Author

Maxine Marsolini has always enjoyed reading, but she didn't set out to be a writer. She divulges to people, "God has an interesting sense of humor." She grew up on a small farm in southern Oregon. After her divorce and remarriage, life became complicated. She found herself as co-captain on a ship headed for mutiny. That began a search for answers to create greater family harmony. While attending Bible Study Fellowship in 1982, she was thrilled to discover God had a lot to say about how we should treat each other and how to use our money. Her blended family began to see that living life as a Christian was having a positive impact on how they acted at home.

All relationships take work and every dollar must be managed. From 1990-2011 Maxine was part of the Crown Financial Ministries leadership team. Now, as the founder of Rebuilding Families www.rebuildingfamilies.net, she shares the wisdom gleaned over the years with others, fully believing that, when the right helps are accompanied by prayer, everyone can reach their highest God-given potential.

Other books by Maxine include:

- Blended Families

- Raising Children in Blended Families
- Rebuilding Families One Dollar at A Time
- Blended Families Workbook

You can find her tried and tested ideas in articles appearing in magazines, blogs, and compilation books. She is considered a valuable resource for family matters. As co-host of *The River*, blog talk radio, she interviews authors and leaders among outreach ministries and experts on current topics. www.blogtalkradio.com/krvr

Maxine received life coach training at Western Seminary and is a lay member of the American Association of Christian Counselors. She currently serves as president of the Oregon Christian Writers www.oregonchristianwriters.org, and holds membership in the DAR (Daughters of the American Revolution), and the National Association of Professional Women. She loves to spend time enjoying family, friends, travel adventures and taking morning walks with a little white dog named Sophie. Through it all, she's learned to be thankful for each new sunrise and God's creative sense of humor.